TEEN·OLOGY

Books by
Jim Burns
FROM BETHANY HOUSE PUBLISHERS

Closer (with Cathy Burns)

*Confident Parenting**

*Creating an Intimate Marriage**

Teenology

PURE FOUNDATIONS

Accept Nothing Less

God Made Your Body

How God Makes Babies

The Purity Code

Teaching Your Children Healthy Sexuality†

*Audio CD; DVD & Curriculum Kit also available

†Parents' Kit also available: *The Purity Code,
Teaching Your Children Healthy Sexuality,*
and special Audio Resource CD

JIM BURNS, PhD

TEEN·OLOGY

THE ART OF RAISING GREAT TEENAGERS

BETHANYHOUSE

MINNEAPOLIS, MINNESOTA

Published by Bethany House Publishers
11400 Hampshire Avenue South
Bloomington, Minnesota 55438

Bethany House Publishers is a division of
Baker Publishing Group, Grand Rapids, Michigan.

Printed in the United States of America

In keeping with biblical principles of creation stewardship, Baker Publishing Group advocates the responsible use of our natural resources. As a member of the Green Press Initiative, our company uses recycled paper when possible. The text paper of this book is comprised of 30% post-consumer waste.

 green press INITIATIVE

Library of Congress Cataloging-in-Publication Data

Burns, Jim.
    Teenology : the art of raising great teenagers / Jim Burns.
        p. cm.
    Includes bibliographical references.
    Summary: "Christian teen expert offers a candid and comprehensive guide to raising today's teens"—Provided by publisher.
    ISBN 978-0-7642-0704-4 (pbk. : alk. paper) 1. Parent and teenager—Religious aspects—Christianity. 2. Parenting—Religious aspects—Christianity. 3. Teenagers—Religious life. 4. Child rearing—Religious aspects—Christianity. I. Title.
    BV4529.B873   2010
    248.8'45—dc22

                                                                    2010021632

To Doug Fields

One of my youth group kids who has become the
foremost leader in the world of youth ministry.
A friend and partner in ministry whom I deeply
respect and admire.

Acknowledgments

Thank you . . .

Cathy Burns . . . for your amazing partnership in life and ministry. Thank you for your patience with the writing of this book and for your care and love through this season of life. I am the world's most fortunate man.

Christy, Rebecca, and Heidi Burns . . . daughters who bring me joy every day of my life, even if you thought I was a nerd when you were teens.

Cindy Ward . . . you are a gift from God.

David Peck, Jon Wallace, and Dave Bixby . . . This partnership with the HomeWord Center for Youth and Family at Azusa Pacific University is a dream come true. I can't think of anyone or any other organization in the universe I would rather work with to change the world.

Rod Emery and Randy Bramel . . . You didn't have to do so much and yet you do. I literally thank God for you every day.

Tic Long, Wayne Rice, and the late Mike Yaconelli . . . You believed in a young, wet-behind-the-ears youth worker and gave me the chance to speak to the world through Youth Specialties. I am so grateful.

Kyle Duncan, Natasha Sperling, and Jeff Braun . . . Your ability to edit and publish is major league all-star level. Your willingness to show grace to broken deadlines has ministered to me more than you will ever imagine.

Roger, Mary, Jim, Susan, Sue, Ben, Ted, and Judy . . . I love coming to work, and I know you sacrifice every day for the people who will read this book and so many others. Some of those people may never get to meet you, but you have touched their lives like you do mine.

Greg Johnson . . . You rock as an agent and you are now a friend for life. You are appreciated and valued.

Contents

Introduction

In a way, you are holding my life's work in your hands. I have written other books, but a book is like a child. You love each one uniquely. This book, though, represents a lifelong passion. Or at least a passion that started when I was sixteen.

Before that, I was the kid who knew exactly what I was going to do when I grew up. While childhood friends wanted to be a fireman one day and a doctor the next, I wanted just one thing: to be a professional baseball player, like my brother.

Baseball was my passion. Then, a few months after my sixteenth birthday, I was hanging out with friends at the beach over Easter vacation when a stranger handed me a piece of paper with a photo of the ocean and a Psalm written on it. Something stirred within me, and I moved from wanting to be a baseball player to wanting to help teenagers. Some people would say it was a sign from God. Back then I wouldn't have said that. However, in hindsight I do think it was part of a calling on my life. And I have never wanted to do anything else. Even when I speak at marriage conferences or write books to parents, the ultimate reason is to help kids.

I started helping teens right after that Easter experience, and I haven't stopped since. As an adult, I would even sit at the "kid table" at the Burns' family Christmas parties. I love teenagers.

Because of my work with teenagers and their families, I thought this would be an easy book to write. Was I ever wrong. I have rewritten entire chapters, changed topics, moved paragraphs, and generally struggled with what to say. Parenting teens is not easy, especially with the tough things kids are facing today. Sure, the technological advances and opportunities are amazing, yet teens have to deal with Internet pornography, terrorism threats, and so many experiences that didn't exist that day I felt called to work with teens. Some teens are making amazing decisions to commit their lives to make this world a better place. Others are lost and overwhelmed. I didn't want this message to be depressing. But at the same time, I wanted to be a realist. Life is complicated for teens and for their parents. I didn't want to give easy, trite answers to complex issues, and at the same time I wanted to create a very hopeful book.

It was interesting to hear the responses when I told parents I was writing a book on raising teenagers. I usually got a sigh, a rolling of the eyes, and that far-off look that said, "I need this book!" My wife, Cathy, and I know the feeling. Our three daughters are through the teen years now and on to what I describe in this book as "emerging adulthood." I look back at their adolescence with a fondness for the ride we were on while also remembering the sheer terror that they might make poor choices that would last a lifetime. One thing I know—and what you will read from me—is you will be a much more effective parent of a teen if you stay calm, develop a plan that you follow, and then get as emotionally healthy as you possibly can. If you like roller coaster rides, get ready for the ride of your life.

Jim Burns, PhD
Dana Point, California

PART ONE

Parenting Teens to Become Responsible Adults

ONE

Who Is That Stranger in Your House?

Three things amaze me,
no, four things I'll never understand—
how an eagle flies so high in the sky,
how a snake glides over a rock,
how a ship navigates the ocean,
why adolescents act the way they do.

Proverbs 30:18–19 (The Message)

It has been said that raising kids is part joy and part guerrilla warfare. And during the teen years? Everything is intensified. I have spent my entire adult life focused on helping teens and their parents navigate adolescence, yet I don't have many easy answers. There is hope and practical help for you in this book, but there is no such thing as a quick fix or a magic potion when it comes to raising a teenager.

Free small-group guides for each chapter of *Teenology* are available at *www .HomeWord.com/teenologysmallgroupcurriculum.*

Perhaps it's not easy helping teens become responsible adults because adolescence, as we know it, is a relatively new phenomenon. The term *teenager* was first introduced to the world in 1941 in, of all magazines, *Popular Science*. The American high school is less than a hundred years old. Even in some cultures today, the transition from child to adult takes place at thirteen years old (or puberty), and the "teenage" years are completely skipped. Can you imagine your young teen taking on adult responsibilities today?

Personally, Cathy and I have been humbled by raising our three strong-willed daughters. We have dealt with our share of hormones, drama, chaos, and confusion. More than once I asked myself, "Am I crazy and they're normal, or am I normal and they're crazy?" My mistake was thinking that raising a compliant, self-reliant teenager might be difficult for others but not for me. After all, some people were already calling me an expert in the field of adolescence those days. That's not how my kids saw it, though. I still remember driving with my middle daughter, Rebecca, who was sixteen at the time, when she blurted out, "You know, Dad, all my friends think you are the coolest dad they know." She went on to tell me what the kids said about me, and my head grew to astronomical proportions. Then I made the big mistake.

"So do you think I'm a cool dad?"

Her answer came swiftly. "No. You won't change my curfew. Everyone else gets to see movies that you won't let me see. Everybody else wears clothes that you won't let me wear." Summing it all up, she added, "They just don't know how mean and strict you can be."

Ouch.

Then somehow, after delivering these death blows to

my shaky ego, she calmly asked, "Dad, can you take me to the shoe store to buy some new flats after we get a frozen yogurt?"

A dog trainer once told us that training your dog is 66 percent human training and 33 percent actual dog training. I think the same rings true for raising teenagers.

Here is what I am going to say in this book to you:

"Stay calm. Adolescence is a temporary transition. Work your plan. Hold on to your seat belt. Get as emotionally, physically, and spiritually healthy as you possibly can, and before you know it, that sweet kid who morphed into a teen and sometimes hates you will become a responsible adult."

There is hope. Even teens that do bad things can turn out okay. To one extent or another, all teens are moving from dependence on the parents toward independence. One of the deepest cries of adolescence is FREEDOM, and it's the parents' job to help their teen become a responsible adult. We can only do that when we move our parenting role from controlling to consulting and from micromanaging to mentoring. Some authors call this giving your teenager roots and wings. This roots and wings idea is not always easy for your teen because they seem to be more interested in the wings part. On the other hand, we parents still want to hold on to the roots. And often for a good reason, because when you give your teenager their wings, they stumble and fall or fly in the wrong direction. It's complicated.

We can only do that when we move our parenting role from controlling to consulting and from micromanaging to mentoring.

THE HEART OF A PARENT

You may be reading this book because you are trying to figure out how to reach that stranger in your house. Wasn't it just yesterday that they would snuggle up to you and it seemed like they lived to please you? Now there are days (maybe weeks and months) when it appears they can't stand you or what you stand for in life. During a particularly rough time with one of my daughters, I bought her a blank card that had an ocean and palm tree on the front. Inside I wrote a quote by Maureen Hawkins that perfectly described Cathy's and my feelings: *"Before you were conceived I wanted you. Before you were born I loved you. Before you were a minute old, I would have died for you. This is the miracle of life."*

Somehow the moment you have a child, part of your heart is ripped out of you and placed in the heart of that child and you are never the same. A late-night phone call when one of our kids wasn't home always caused anxiety. A cough, a fever, a sports injury would bring panic and worry. A poor decision about morals and values would cause terror in my soul. For years I thought I was alone with these feelings or just had too weak of a faith, but as I started expressing these emotions to friends, they agreed that the love we have for our child is like no other love. I have sat with parents who have lost their child in an accident or from cancer. The hurt and brokenness often runs deeper than even the loss of a spouse or a parent.

Many couples say the most difficult time in their marriage was during the teen years of their children. There were disagreements on how to set boundaries, little time was spent focused on the marriage, and if the kids were rebelling there was an incredible amount of guilt and tension on the part of the parents. One evening after a seminar and hearing an unusually difficult amount of painful stories from parents of teens, I remember coming home to my wife and saying, "The teen years are causing parents, especially moms, to be emotional basket cases." There is more stress in this generation of American families than in any previous generation, and it is playing havoc on the emotional health of parents. Raising kids was not meant to be this difficult.

THE PRIVATE LIFE OF THE TEENAGER

Parents aren't the only ones who are struggling. Teens are also going through tremendous changes. I was interviewing film producer Michael Landon Jr. on our HomeWord radio broadcast, and he flatly stated, "This is the first generation of young people who have experienced the complete death of innocence."[1] Just this past month I looked out at a large crowd of teenagers I was speaking to and said, "I wouldn't want to be your age."

This generation likely has to deal with viewing Internet pornography by age eleven and cell phone "sexting"[2] in middle school. In fact, our parents probably were upset with our use of the home telephone line, but your children's cell phone will be the greatest provider of pornography for their generation. Add the pressure to conform to the cultural norm of the day and society's sheer lack of a biblical worldview, and it is no wonder kids are struggling. Today's teens face more violence, promiscuity, drug abuse, and depression than any previous generation. And issues like sexual abuse, eating disorders, self-injury, and sexually transmitted diseases are at a mind-boggling, epidemic scale. Sure, these problems were around when we were growing up, but not to the extent they are now and not at the age of our kids. We were twelve, fourteen, and seventeen, but we were never their age. They experience so much so young.

Most families are trying to manage the teen years without a strategy in place. Many couples are not on the same page and single parents have never had it so hard. I am not by nature a negative person, but the private life of the American teenager has never been so complicated.

The good news is, these challenges are causing parents and experts in the field to rethink how to help teens survive and thrive in a world turned upside down. Some kids will be affected harder than others. Some, who in elementary school looked like they would breeze through their teen years without a hitch, will be in a battle and others will waltz through adolescence unscathed. But with a plan and purpose, you can help your teen navigate this season in his or her life. The first step is making sure we have a realistic view of healthy teenagers and their parents.

With a plan and purpose, you can help your teen navigate this season in his or her life.

WHAT DOES A HEALTHY TEEN LOOK LIKE?

I love the comic strip that shows a teen racing into the living room and announcing to her parents that she just left the kitchen a mess. We see a blown-up macaroni cup in the microwave and a spilled diet soda on the counter. The girl tells her mom she needs her black jeans washed for tomorrow and then begs her dad to borrow his car because hers is low on gas. She lets them know her home-work isn't done and she can't find her cell phone, but she has to run because she is late for a date with her friends at the mall . . . uh, library. As she leaves, she asks, "Where's my other shoe?" The mom looks up from her magazine and tells her husband, "Just think: When we are old, she may be the one taking care of us." He responds with only a look of fright.

What does a healthy teenager look like? What exactly is normal teen behavior? The controversial Sigmund Freud once suggested that adolescence is a temporary mental ill-ness. His daughter, Anna Freud, who followed in her father's vocational footsteps, said, "To be normal during the adoles-cent period is by itself abnormal."[3] Much more recently, Walt Mueller, my good friend and an adolescent culture expert, described adolescence as a transitional stage in which your child is "an adult trying to happen."[4]

When you think of the teen years, words like *emotional roller coaster, pimples, phone, drama, chaos, extreme laughter, extreme anger, extreme emotion, extreme everything!, pushing the limits, drawing outside the lines, rebellion, experimentation, attitude, frustration,* and *passion* are all important parts of the mix. What part of a teen's life isn't changing? Not only are there massive physical changes, but emotions are run-ning wild, and once-nice ten-year-olds become insufferably argumentative. Cathy and I often asked each other, "Who is that person now living in our house?" And just when we thought we had it semi–figured out, the next child came along and brought us the "gift" of a totally different way of dealing with her teenage years.

Self-Identity

One primary task in the teenage years is to form a sense of self-identity. This is why your kid may move from one peer group to another or change styles of clothes or music or friends or . . . you fill in the blank. In reality, teens are searching for their identity. For many parents, the worry is that if their kid doesn't find a sense of healthy identity by age eighteen, they may never find it. We all know adults who are still trying to find themselves and continue to make unwise decisions. If only it was so easy as the couple whose college-aged son announced he was going to quit school to find himself. The dad replied, "What's the point of taking time off to find out who you are when your mother and I can just tell you?"

Healthy Relationships

Relationships mean everything to teens. And, as you well know, friendships influence them for good and for bad. The teenage years are when, hopefully, they develop meaningful, healthy relationships. If that doesn't happen, adulthood relationships can get rather messy. Adolescence is the season where peer pressure can cause problems in the decision-making process of a rather healthy young person. That's why I tell parents to continue to get to know their teen's friends. Peer pressure isn't always negative. It can be positive, so I am a strong proponent of church youth group involvement. Encouraging kids to spend time around positive kids in a healthy environment is always a good idea. Here is a proverb to live by: "Walk with the wise and become wise; associate with fools and get into trouble" (Proverbs 13:20).

Good Decisions

Teenagers today are making decisions that will affect them for the rest of their lives. A healthy teen is not going to make perfect decisions every time, but they do need to realize that even at their age decisions count. Too many young people are not equipped to make good decisions, and they tragically move toward drug and alcohol abuse, porn addiction, poor choices about school, and the list goes on. Hoping to avoid problems, some parents step in and try to make every decision—big and small—for their teen. But that won't help a child mature. When teens learn that life is filled with the pain of discipline vs. the pain of regret, it will help them greatly with wise decision making.

Developing a Relationship With God

A major reason I have focused my vocational purpose on young people is because the teen years are a critical period for developing a relationship with God. In the teen years you often see kids leave their parents' faith to find their own. Authorities tell us that 85 percent of the commitments to Jesus Christ are by people younger than eighteen years old. A healthy young person won't have all their faith development issues worked out, but they will be open to searching for God's best in their life. At the same time, the teen years are the experimental years where they believe in God today but tomorrow they may doubt. This is just a normal part of growing up. Parents are by far the most influential part of their child's faith development. Yet most parents feel inadequately prepared to help direct their children's faith development.[5]

So part of normal healthy teenage development is

- Finding a healthy self identity
- Establishing healthy relationships
- Making good decisions
- Developing a relationship with God

Of course, young people are working through these issues and others, all in the context of change, experimentation, and a great desire for freedom, which brings their parents to a very challenging season of their own.

WHAT DOES A HEALTHY PARENT OF A TEEN LOOK LIKE?

Today, when adolescent specialists get together, it is not unusual for them to spend more time and concern on parenting issues than on the teens themselves. There has been an extreme shift in the parenting styles of moms and dads, not to mention the culture in which our kids are living. Unfortunately, far too many parents of teens are emotionally and even spiritually unhealthy. One mom told me she has a recurring dream that her child is falling off a cliff, just out of her reach. The dream isn't necessarily unhealthy, but it may show how much parents worry about saving their kids from the world's problems.

My good friend, mentor, and parenting expert John Rosemond coined the term "helicopter parent" to describe parents who are risking their own marriage, physical health, and self-image by hovering over their children and over-parenting them. In a recent HomeWord radio interview, Rosemond said, "Too many parents are ultimately carrying the heavy burdens of their teen's problems on their own shoulders." No teen will become a responsible adult if their parents carry the load for them. It's not healthy for either party.

So what do healthy parents of teens look like? These parents take their God-given role of parenting seriously and act like a leader. Leaders lead the way, but they don't carry the other person's baggage. Leaders teach their children self-management skills. They consult but don't control, because control freaks are really never in control. Leaders help children learn to discern right values and teach them about sexual purity (more on this in chapter 5). Parents who act like leaders also create inviting home environments with plenty of connection, fun, and creativity.

No teen will become a responsible adult if their parents carry the load for them.

One important aspect of parent-leadership is making sure you have enough margin in your life to have the energy to lead. Often, parents are running around so ragged that there is nothing left but emotional scraps for their families.

Bill Hybels advises fellow pastors to invest at least 50 percent of their leadership energy on themselves. If that sounds selfish or self-centered, the reality is that parents need to do the same and take care of themselves. We parents must allow our children to deal with the consequences of their own decisions. Someone once told me, "Untended fires soon become nothing but a pile of ashes." I know if I am not tending my own soul care, I am a poor excuse of a father and a lousy husband.

Healthy couples also make sure they make time for each other. Just this week I was giving a parenting seminar and asked the people, "What percent of your time are you a mom or a dad, and what percent of your time are you a wife or a husband?" The answer was enlightening: about 90 percent time as a parent and 10 percent as a spouse. A child-focused lifestyle isn't healthy, and frankly, it's not fair to the kids if you expect to be a healthy role model. So it's back to what I said at the beginning of the chapter: Parents have to stay calm, get on the same page to work their plan, and then stay as emotionally and spiritually healthy as they possibly can.

THE CAT YEARS

Our family has raised dogs and cats over the years. Today, we have two incredibly compliant and loving golden retrievers, Hobie and Kona. We have also had our share of cats. At the risk of offending cat lovers, I like dogs more than cats. Dogs are loyal, affectionate, and easy to train, and they love to please. On the other hand, my experience with cats is that although they can be affectionate and loving (sort of), it is almost always on their terms. Dogs come bounding up to you with a smile (do dogs really smile?) and offer you their head to be petted and loved on. A cat has to be in the right mood. If you wait long enough, the cat just might curl up on your lap, but it usually takes a while.

I've heard people compare dogs to young children and cats to teens. Cats have minds of their own. They give you blank stares, as if they don't know you or don't want to know you. They leave the home, sometimes for long periods. They seem more preoccupied with their needs and wants. They hardly ever want to do anything with the family. Micromanaging a cat rarely works and just brings more frustration. Cats mope around and sometimes look almost depressed.

Sure, sometimes they give you love and attention. But if you act surprised, it is almost as if they look at you and wonder why. Tell a cat to sit and it jumps on the sofa. The more you smother a cat, the quicker it moves away from you. But with a little patience and even some gentle affection, cats eventually come around. After all, they need love and nurturing too.

Yes, one day your teenager will grow up and visit you. He will greet you with enthusiasm and affection. He will walk right over to the counter, make you some tea, and ask about your day. Then you will realize that your cat is a dog again.

TWO

Correcting Behavior Without Crushing Character

He who is carried on another man's back does not appreciate how far the town is.

African Proverb

Shaun comes in to my office with his parents. It's the last place Shaun wants to be, especially with his parents! His mom and dad, on the other hand, are hopeful that something good will come from our conversation. Mostly, though, they are emotionally shattered. His mom is close to tears before she starts talking. Shaun's dad is quiet, pensive, a bit removed. I sense he has had it with Shaun, and probably with his wife too. She tells me her life is in turmoil and that she doesn't feel supported by her husband. She thinks he takes a backseat when it comes to discipline and setting boundaries with Shaun. For a moment I think they need marriage counseling more than advice about Shaun. But then again, that's the case with a lot of couples who are raising teenagers today.

Shaun seems to be a typical adolescent who is going through an extreme experimental phase. He is doing poorly in school, talks back to his parents, has a horrible attitude, and is generally disobedient and rude at home. As his mom talks, he slouches more and more. Of the three of them, Shaun is wearing the least stress on his countenance. The funny thing is, I sort of like Shaun. I can tell he "gets it" but is choosing to rebel. Yes, he is mixed up and not being obedient, but in my heart I can just feel that he isn't as bad as his mom claims.

My guess from our conversation is that Shaun has been indulged by overprotective parents. He has a bit of "entitlement king" going on and he isn't going to get with the program until he feels some pain. Someone once told me, "When the pain of remaining the same is greater than the pain of changing, you will change." It's back to the pain of discipline or the pain of regret philosophy. Shaun hasn't felt much pain of regret yet, and he definitely isn't disciplined in ways his parents hope for him. He doesn't have the internal motivation to improve, and the external motivation from his parents doesn't seem to be working.

Shaun's mom goes on about his poor grades, poor attitude, poor friendships, and lack of desire for spiritual growth as well as a host of decisions having to do with morals and values. She is overwhelmed. After listening to her, I think we all are. I think to myself, *Wow. This woman is carrying it all on her back.* She then goes after her husband and his lack of leadership in the home. He gets mad and defensive and tells me, "I *am* concerned about Shaun. He's wasting his potential, but she starts acting crazy." Shaun nods his head in agreement. I feel the mom's pain—my three strong-willed kids didn't always walk the straight and narrow path. Shaun yearns for freedom. But it seems like the more freedom he takes, the poorer the choices he makes. Mom is digging in her heels and wants control.

The freedom/control cycle is common in homes with teenagers. As kids move from dependence on their parents toward independence, this freedom/control cycle doesn't usually come easy. Even in the healthiest of families, teenagers aren't ready for complete freedom. But little by little, parents must give up control on their teenager's life so the teen will eventually enjoy responsible adulthood.

By the time it's my turn to talk, our time is almost up. I am hopeful these relationships can be salvaged. But it is going to take responsible decision making not just from Shaun, but from Mom and Dad as well. I turn in my chair toward the parents and take about fifteen seconds of silence to get their attention. The pause feels like a long time, but I want my initial words to count. "You are taking on all of Shaun's poor choices. You need to take that monkey off your back and place it squarely where it belongs—on his back."

GET THE MONKEY OFF YOUR BACK

Micromanaging parents never get the results they hope for, and most often they end up disappointed. The most effective parents are those who surrender the control they really don't have and offer choices for their teens to make. That is the way to teach responsibility and respect.

For high school senior Lindsey and her parents, the freedom/control cycle was centered on homework. An incredibly bright girl, Lindsey just didn't apply herself to her homework.

Her parents would nag, bribe, restrict, shame, and sometimes even do her homework themselves, all so she could keep her grades up and get a college scholarship. Finally, they took Lindsey's lack-of-discipline monkey off their backs and placed it on hers. They sat down with her and explained that they were partly at fault for all the tension in the home. They admitted that by her age they should be nagging less. Starting then, they would release the homework decisions to her. She alone would experience the consequences of her academic decisions. It was a good talk, but that doesn't mean things changed right away. Lindsey continued to miss homework assignments, and her grades weren't good enough to get into a four-year university. But two years at a community college did bring some maturity to her thinking, and she eventually became an excellent student, graduating with honors from UCLA.

The responsibilities of growing up shouldn't all rest on the shoulders of parents. We have to let our teens go and let them grow. The most valuable lessons in life often come as consequences from making a mistake. Before freedom often comes pain. If we parents continue to indulge and enable our teenagers, we are helping to create irresponsible kids who are not going to grow up to become responsible adults.

One woman told me, "Our son has everything. I just don't understand why his grades and behavior are so bad." Smile. She was missing the point. Because she indulged her child, why on earth would he want to take on the responsibility needed to make better decisions? Plus, I feel sorry for his future wife. If he doesn't receive some responsibility soon, he will not be able to make healthy, responsible decisions as an adult.

UNITED WE STAND AND DIVIDED WE FALL

When it comes to discipline and boundaries, parents must try to be proactive and take a united stand. Of course, this isn't easy. No two people parent exactly alike. There will be disagreements, and much of the marital conflict through the teen years does center on setting boundaries and handing out discipline. Sometimes the father is far too strict. He isn't a good day-to-day disciplinarian, and then all of a sudden out of anger he lowers the boom and scares everyone in the family with his temper and his threats. Or Dad is just the opposite—he is the Disneyland dad who lets the kids get away with most anything to bring peace to the household. Moms are typically more involved in the day-to-day discipline of the kids, and they are the same people who get frustrated with their husbands or ex-husbands for not going along with the program.

The easiest way to get on the same page as parents is to keep the goal in front of you: to build up your children's character and to help them become responsible adults. Your goal should not be simply making them happy or being their best friend. When a parent tries to be buddy-buddy with his or her child, typically out of the parent's own need, the parent-child relationship falls apart. Be the parent.

When a parent tries to be buddy-buddy with his or her child, typically out of the parent's own need, the parent-child relationship falls apart. Be the parent.

Bill Cosby once said he didn't know the secret to success, but he knew the secret of failure is trying to keep everybody happy all the time. When your kids get through their teen years, hopefully you can enter a very fulfilling period of mentorship and mutual care. But until then, parents need to stay consistent about discipline and character building. This is most difficult for single moms and dads who have been through a rough divorce or even death. It's not uncommon for teens to reject their parents in some way, and this is just too tough emotionally for a parent who already has major bruises from other relationships.

Getting on the same page means developing a philosophy of parenting that both parents can agree to, and then, as I said before, staying calm, working the plan, and doing what you can to be emotionally healthy and moving forward.[1] I often suggest couples read a book together or take a parenting class. Why is it that we will hire a personal trainer to help us get in shape or read books on diet or nutrition, but relatively few of us will read a book on parenting, go to a seminar, or seek counseling to improve our skills?

A few years ago I challenged some men to read one marriage book and one parenting book each year. They always seemed to find time to read materials to improve their business skills, but until the challenge, none of the men had read a single book on family issues. I hardly ever include e-mails in my books, but I want to share what one man wrote:

> I took you up on your challenge to get on the same page with my wife. She had been bugging me to read a parenting book and go to a marriage conference at our church. After hearing your message I told my wife I would read that book and go to "her" conference. Guess what? The only thing I can say is that the book and marriage conference revolutionized my life. I had always put energy into my work, and figured my wife could do the reading and attending for both of us. I spent time with the kids and tried to help, but I realized quickly that she was doing the

heavy lifting in our parenting and our marriage. This year we have been much more together and it has been wonderful. Thanks for helping me change my way of thinking and change my life.

It takes time, energy, and intentionality to get on the same page as your spouse, but it will keep you from being divided and always parenting in a reactive mode.

LEAD WITH LOVE, PURPOSE, AND AUTHORITY

I'm afraid too many parents have indulged and enabled their children to such an extent that they have helped create irresponsible and even narcissistic kids. When we have weak, inconsistent discipline and poor boundaries, kids just aren't willing to grow up. This doesn't mean teens shouldn't be nurtured and affirmed, though. Every child needs parents who can be irrationally positive toward them. Yet at the same time, they need us to express expectations, set high standards, and hold them accountable. In other words, our kids need us to lead.

Leaders are consistent with their discipline and consistently express clear expectations. Discipline is fundamentally a matter of leadership. I have spoken to and studied leaders in all fields of life. One thing they 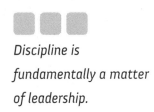 *Discipline is fundamentally a matter of leadership.* have in common is consistency with their message. They role model what they expect and then they keep on task. With an excellent leader there is seldom a doubt about who is in charge and the purpose for what they are doing. Even though all parents aren't business leaders, they are the leaders of their home. The question in many homes of rebellious teenagers is "Who's in charge?" This question must be settled with everyone in the home, and the only healthy answer is that the parents must take the lead. Inconsistency or poor role modeling or guidance will place your kids in a leadership position that isn't healthy for anyone.

What does leadership mean? It means a parent must eliminate any power struggle from the relationship. Resolve the authority issues. I tell people almost every week in parenting seminars, "Don't argue and don't fight with your kids." It is way too difficult to mentor and lead if you and your children are fighting and arguing all the time.

We have a daughter who could win most of the arguments in our home. She is dynamic and articulate and can argue either side of an issue. When she was a teenager she liked to argue for the sake of arguing and stretched the boundaries whenever possible. There were times she was just exhausting. Then one day a therapist friend gave us two words of advice: Quit arguing. Cathy and I had to learn to lead. If you think about it, people seldom argue with their leaders. We had to hold our ground and let our daughter know who was boss.

Holding your ground can be wearisome, but it is always worth it (although you probably already know this from your own life experience). To help communicate with our kids about discipline-related issues, Cathy and I came up with what I call "Confident Parenting Talking Points." I wrote about them in greater detail in my book *Confident Parenting*.

1. *"I feel your pain."* If your children know your expectations and they break them, or if they suffer consequences from their poor decisions, let them know you care and that you feel their pain. You have empowered

your teenager to make healthy decisions, but if she doesn't do that, you can show her empathy while holding her accountable. In a recent HomeWord radio broadcast, John Rosemond shared what he told his kids: "If I was your age, I'd feel the same way. The answer is still no, but you are doing a great job expressing yourself."

2. *"Nevertheless."* This might be the most important word in the English language to show our kids who really is the leader. Yes, we do feel their pain and we are listening; *nevertheless,* the consequences are going to stay. Adapting John's words to his kids, I'd say, "I can understand how you feel, and I might have felt the same way when I was your age. Nevertheless . . ."

3. *"Life isn't fair."* The sooner your kids understand that life isn't fair, and that whining and complaining won't get them what they want, they will quit trying the make-it-fair game. Whenever you can, let reality be the teacher for your kids. If whining and manipulating works for a child, even some of the time, it is the parent who has to live with the consequences. Here are some more wise words John Rosemond shared in one of our radio broadcasts together: "Parents should not agonize over what a child fails to do or does, if the child is perfectly capable of agonizing over it themself." Whatever your child's age, it's about time they learn the truth that life isn't always fair, but it sure can be good.

DEVELOPING CHARACTER AND RESPONSIBILITY

One major issue during the teen years is rebellion. In one way or another, all teens rebel. It's in their job description. Some teens take their rebellion into very self-destructive directions, while others test their parents just enough to make them uncomfortable.

In one way or another, all teens rebel. It's in their job description.

Adolescence is the time for your children to seek independence as they separate from you. Don't take this desire for freedom as a blow to you or your parenting. It is the normal cycle of becoming a responsible adult. So if you are looking for close bonding with your teenager, it may not happen.

One of the ironies of parenting is that we have to give our kids the freedom to fail in order for them to grow up. If you over-parent your teenager and become a helicopter parent, your actions are shouting to your teen that you don't believe she can succeed by herself. We must go through the process of releasing our kids so they can move toward responsibility. A person who never learns to take full responsibility for their life and actions will never have the chance to develop healthy character and be fully happy.

Foster Cline, in his excellent book *Parenting Teens with Love and Logic*, offers four steps toward responsibility:

- Step 1. Give your teen responsibility.

- Step 2. Trust that your child will carry it out and at the same time hope and pray that they will blow it. (They will learn from their misstep.)

- Step 3. When she does blow it, stand back and allow consequences to occur while expressing empathy.

- Step 4. Turn right back around and give him the same responsibility all over again, because that sends a powerful implied message: "You're so smart that you can learn. People do learn from their mistakes, and you're no different."[2]

The more times parents can offer their kids empathy for mistakes along the way the better. For example, when grades are suffering, the appropriate response is, "I hope you will still be able to figure out how to pay the extra money for car insurance until your good student discount kicks back in when you improve your grades." Part of teaching responsibility and character is holding your kids accountable for their actions. That's why it's important to express your expectations. The fewer surprises the better. Again, remember that the most valuable lessons in life come from the consequence of making a mistake. Let reality be the teacher.

EXPECTATIONS AND THE FAMILY CONTRACT

Much unhealthy rebellion and misbehavior can be slowed down if parents are proactive rather than reactive. A proactive parent will take the time and invest the energy to clearly express their expectations to their kids. If things are still not working, then it's time to put together a family contract.

If things are still not working, then it's time to put together a family contract.

A family contract involves literally putting on paper a plan with expectations and consequences for behavior. It is always best to create the contract together with your child, and never in the heat of the battle. For example, for years in the Burns household we had problems with kids delaying their homework assignments. We found that nagging, lecturing, grounding, and generally creating a negative environment just didn't work. It only made us all miserable. The homework monkey on the back was getting passed around to all of us, so we decided to develop a contract with the girls' help. Sitting at a Starbucks, in a casual environment with as little emotion as possible, seemed to work best for us when discussing a contract and expectations.

When putting together a contract, keep it as simple as possible. Here is a simple outline to follow:

A Family Contract

Issue:
Expectations:
Accountability:
Positive Consequences:
Negative Consequences:

These five questions (and sample answers) can help:

1. What is the issue? (Lack of discipline with homework.)

2. What is a reasonable expectation with your homework? (An ideal response: *Complete it in a timely manner!*)

3. How can we hold you accountable? (Daily homework check-in with one of the parents at an agreed-upon time.)

4. What are the rewards for a job well done? (List out things like *a sense of accomplishment, feeling good about myself,* and *college preparation* as well as perhaps a

material reward of buying a new outfit or celebrating with Dad at a ball game.)

5. What are the consequences if you do not meet the expectations? (Things like *unable to go to a four-year college right out of high school, poor grades,* and *costly car insurance* as well as immediate practical consequences like no computer time until the homework is done, driving privileges or sports activities removed.)

Parents sometimes need a tool such as a family contract. Shame-based parenting never works in the long haul. And preaching, criticizing, and yelling are never effective at motivating. They tend to close your child's spirit toward you. With a contract, however, children learn to discipline themselves and become more obedient. It's a parent's job to maximize character and responsibility, and we do that best by evoking discipline and boundaries. Responsible and obedient kids are the happiest kids. By and large, most teens do want to succeed and, believe it or not, please their parents.

NEVER GIVE UP

The bottom line of building character and responsibility into your teen's life is that there is hope. Even if you are in the pit of adolescent hormones, drama, and rebellion, know that most teens do make it through this stage. It's just a phase between childhood and adulthood. The truth to hold on to is that teens can be rude, selfish, and rebellious and still turn out just fine. Teens can make poor choices and experiment with poor behavior and still grow up okay. Your teen might do things you will never know about, or at least not for years to come, and really can become a responsible adult of character.

Too many parents are emotional wrecks because they are carrying the weight of their child's behavior on their back. No matter how good of a parent you are, your child is quite capable of making poor choices and horrible decisions. Proper discipline does not always guarantee proper behavior. However, if you develop and carry out a parenting plan—while getting as emotionally, spiritually, and physically healthy as possible yourself—you and your teen will have a much better chance of leading healthy, fulfilling lives.

Cathy and I have felt our share of tremors living in earthquake country in Southern California. When the San Francisco earthquake hit in 1989, we were speaking at an event in the Hyatt Regency ballroom. Talk about a unique experience. The damage in the Bay Area was devastating and the loss was terrible. However, that same year an even worse earthquake occurred on the other side of the world in what was then called Soviet Armenia. In minutes, the nation was flattened and over thirty thousand people lost their lives. Moments after the quake stopped, a father rushed to his son's elementary school and found it completely leveled to the ground. Not sure what to do, he remembered a promise he had made to his son: "No matter what happens, I will always be there for you." The desperate father began to dig through the rubble where he thought his son's classroom might have been.

As other parents arrived, sobbing for their children, the father kept digging. After several frantic hours, his wife came to his side and quietly said, "Our son is dead. Let's go home to the other children, mourn our loss, and rebuild our home." But the father refused to quit. After more than twenty-four hours of searching, with his energy waning and his hands raw, he pulled back a huge boulder and heard his son's voice. "Armand!" he screamed. "Is that you?" And the voice answered, "Dad, it's me. I told the kids not to worry. I told them if you were alive, you'd save me and then they'd be saved too. I told them your promise to always be there for me."[3]

More than anything else, your kids need to know you will be there for them. You don't want to necessarily bail them out. That won't bring character and responsibility. But in the midst of what can be turbulent adolescent years, it's great to reassure your children of your unconditional and sacrificial love. They need this more than anything else. Just as God says to us, "I will never leave you nor forsake you,"[4] you can bring that same reassurance to your children. You can't take away all their problems, but you can walk with them through this most incredible season of life called the teen years.

THREE

Learning the Developmental Stages of Adolescence

"But, Dad, I gotta be a nonconformist," the teenager said to his father. "How else can I be like the other kids?"

Les Parrott

I'm the first to admit it wasn't easy for me when my girls became teenagers. "The change" was not gradual for our kids. Our loving, affectionate, obedient girls suddenly copped attitudes, danced with danger, said and did outrageous things, and weren't very fun to be with some of the time. When I would hear about their antics, my usual response to Cathy was, "Are you kidding me? What were they thinking? I can't believe they did that!" Most of the time it really wasn't horrible stuff, but it floored me how they could be so dangerous, outlandish, or frankly, plain stupid.

These new teens caused me to lose all my confidence as a parent. On top of that, it was clear they didn't like me all that much, and I found I could be mad or disappointed at them 24/7/365. I was the dad who lived on the other side of the generation gap. My kids teased me about my music and clothes and thought my ideas about movies, music, and other media influences were totally out of step with their new teenage reality.

I remember the day I became "not cool" to each of my three daughters. There were different circumstances, but when each reached the age of twelve or so, there was a definite change in the parent-kid relationship. Oh, there were moments away from their friends when I received a bit of affection, but for the most part their move from dependence toward independence involved a huge leap away from Mom and Dad and toward the direction of their friends. As it turned out, these changes were temporary, but I'm not sure I would have believed that back then.

As I've mentioned before, some of this behavior and attitude is absolutely normal for teens on the road toward adulthood. Everything is changing around them. Their bodies are doing things and growing in ways that surprise them. Their minds are changing. Their emotions at times seem to run loose. They are becoming aware of sex and peer pressure and mood swings and rebellion, and they really aren't sure what to do with all of it. On top of that, in their saner moments even they wonder why they act the way they do.

You can partially blame all this on their brains. Honestly. Blame their brains. If your bright and mature teenager has sometimes made some really poor choices, it is partly because their brain, in particular the dorsal lateral prefrontal cortex, won't fully develop until your teen hits their mid-twenties. And this part of the brain plays a critical role in decision making. In fact, without a fully established dorsal lateral prefrontal cortex, even the understanding of future consequences doesn't always function. This is one reason why teen driver crash rates are more than eight times higher than their parents'.

On the outside, teenagers appear to be nearly grown up. But inside the skull, a vital part of their brain is closer to a child's than an adult's. The prefrontal cortex is partly responsible for self-control, judgment, emotional regulation, organization, and even planning. Just like everything else about teenagers, their brains are works in progress.

Just like everything else about teenagers, their brains are works in progress.

When I was in grad school at Princeton, we were taught that during puberty the brain's hardware was completely connected with the last brain growth spurt by age sixteen. Today, we now understand because of magnetic resonance imaging (MRI) that the brain isn't fully developed until age twenty-five. Add a healthy dose of hormones to peer pressure and a brain that doesn't fully function when it comes to being logical about risky behaviors, and you can understand the uniqueness of the teen years.

I realize this idea of your child's brain not being fully developed might not be comforting when you are in the middle of the teen years with your kids, but it does help us make sense of things like poor driving decisions, as well as the drama and emotions of teen life. You can't blame the prefrontal cortex for every dilemma, but I find that the parents who take the time to learn about adolescent development seem to have a better handle on what is going on with those cherished children.

The word that might describe the teen years best is *change*.

It wasn't long ago they were children with childlike minds and bodies, and now they have suddenly morphed into something else. Their bodies might look adult, but their actions are somewhere between child and adult. Let's look at those changes from a developmental standpoint.

PHYSICAL CHANGE

Teens strongly desire their physical appearance to measure up to the cultural norm. Their bodies are getting extreme makeovers, and many feel as if they are wearing a sign around their neck that reads "Caution: New Body Under Construction." Both young men and young women are extremely aware of the changes, but the girls seem to be more vocal about it. Hair is growing where once only skin lived. Sexual organs are growing, or not growing fast enough. Acne seems to feed on the teenage skin and often puts adolescents in an awkward-looking stage. Even muscles and bones are growing, sometimes at an uneven rate. Some kids become very uncoordinated when their body grows six inches over summer vacation, or they become more lethargic because the other aspects of their physical growth haven't caught up with their bodily growth spurt.

All the physical changes often come with awkwardness and comparison. You could have two best girlfriends the exact same age, and one is wearing a training bra and the other looks like she is a young adult. Some guys in their early teens have a mustache and hair on their chest, while other guys are staring daily in the mirror for something to grow out of their chest or armpits. Both tend to be insecure and self-conscious.

Parents need to know that even if the words go unspoken,

most kids are painfully aware of their changing appearance. Kids will play the comparison game and always lose. Our job as parents is to never tease them about their appearance and to reassure them that eventually they will catch up with everyone else— or everyone else will catch up with them. But don't underestimate the pressure of physical appearance and change with your teenager.

Most kids are painfully aware of their changing appearance.

SOCIAL CHANGE

Many parents find themselves totally caught off guard by the power of friends and social development in the teen years. What happened to the child that would rather cuddle with Mom and play with Daddy than anything else in the world? Now their innocent wonder and childlike simplicity is being corrupted by a new view of the world, all through the eyes of their social environment.

Adolescence is a time when they move from a relatively safe environment of a neighborhood and nearby school to a much larger and more impersonal middle school and high school. Teens start making important relationships outside of their family. Hopefully those relationships are healthy, but of course, teens can also make poor decisions about friends and other things. The power of peer pressure can sidetrack even really good kids.

I remember as a seventh grader making a commitment not to drink. I had already seen too much heartache in my family system with alcoholism. However, at Jeanne Crothers' party, Andrew Perez offered me a glass of tequila in front of the most popular kids in the school. When I said no, Andrew responded, "What's the matter, are you chicken?" Well, at that moment my desire to be accepted by my friends was greater than my desire not to drink. So I took the glass and chugged the tequila—not a pleasant experience! But there was no way I would have let any of my friends know that.

Relationships and peer pressure are much more confusing and complicated these days than when we were growing up. Basically, we had fairly well-defined social groups who influenced us. Our parents could keep pretty good track of who our friends were and how they were influencing us. Today, with the world of private cell phones, texting, Facebook, and other networking sites, it is very possible for a parent who is not being proactive to have no idea who their child's best friends and greatest influencers are in real life. My mom was the gatekeeper of all telephone calls to the Burns household and whoever stopped by the house. She knew all. Today, you need to be your teen's friend on Facebook (as I suggest in the next chapter), or you may not know whom she is spending hours with online, on the phone, or via texting. Today's teens still say to their parents the same words we said to our parents, "Everybody is doing it." It is our job as parents to figure out who "everybody" is and how "everybody" is influencing them.

Kids socialize in what is called friendship clusters, and I vote for using almost any way to get to know the people in your teen's cluster of influence without becoming a snoop. In order to be around our kids and their friends, our family added a backyard swimming pool. Among other things, we hosted youth group and Fellowship of Christian Athletes meetings. I'm not suggesting everyone should go into debt to build a pool or go through the amount of furniture and carpet stains we did with hundreds of kids in our house through those years. I am saying that if your house can be a place for kids to hang out, or you are the one who is willing to drive the sports team or dance squad, you will learn more about who is influencing your teen.

EMOTIONAL CHANGE

Few people come out of adolescence without experiencing somewhat intense emotional releases. One dad told me, "I felt like it happened overnight. One day she was my sweet little girl and the next day she was a moody, morose, angry teenager." I would imagine that father will still see glimpses of that sweet girl and she will probably move back to that person as she gets older, but until then, anxiety, worry, anger, self-doubt, passion, and fear can occur with ferocious intensity. There is just too much change going on not to affect the emotions.

Adolescent stress is a growing problem. With the need to navigate more social networks, the pressure to handle boy/girl relationships, parent pressure, and the pressure to keep grades up for a future chance at college, kids are more stressed than any previous generation. Many young people today are making sexual decisions based on emotional involvement that exceeds their maturity level. With an increase in sexual relationships at a younger age, teens and especially young girls are becoming depressed more often. One study revealed that 25 percent of teen girls who had sex became clinically depressed within three months of the experience.

On this roller coaster of emotional ups and downs, you

can be your teen's solid ground. My mom was my safe place. I knew she loved me. She was my biggest cheerleader and a great listener. She took me seriously and did not let the shifting waves of my struggles shock her. The art of listening to our children, especially through their emotional extremes, gives our kids the safe place they need. They don't want Mom and Dad to always rescue them, and they definitely don't want a lecture. Instead, they crave acceptance and approval, dialog, and care.

On this roller coaster of emotional ups and downs, you can be your teen's solid ground.

SPIRITUAL CHANGE

One of the main reasons I remain focused on young people as my life work is because it is such an important time for developing a relationship with God. Most people will make a commitment to Jesus Christ before age eighteen or they never will. It's exciting to see teens explore their spirituality, but it's also a bit scary for us parents. As they move from a concrete faith to a more abstract way of thinking, they just may say and do some things that go against their parents' views. While in college, our daughter Christy felt she had to disown our faith to eventually claim her own faith. Interestingly enough, her faith still looks quite similar to ours.

This is the stage in their faith development where teens may not want to go to church, or they might say things about God just to get you upset. It is a time of passionate belief and passionate doubt. One morning they may sincerely feel called to be a missionary to help starving children, and later in the day they will tell you they don't believe in God anymore and they want nothing to do with church. Both feelings are real, and frankly, for the time being, both feelings are a normal part of their faith development. The worst thing a parent can do is to freak out and panic or say mean things during this time of searching. A majority of young people are on a spiritual quest, and we can't mistake skepticism or doubt as a sign that they are not interested.

Parents must avoid smothering their kids with their own faith. Sure, you can set boundaries ("If you live in our home, we expect you to attend church"), but don't spend much time preaching at them. This will make them run from whatever you are pushing on them. Allow and even affirm the difficult questions. A healthy faith has room for questions. And whenever possible, empower them to put their faith in action. During a tenuous time in the faith development of one of my own daughters, we went on a mission trip together. We served and worked with very poor children in Ecuador. The experience of putting her faith in action caused her to do some very important thinking, and one month after college graduation, she moved to Ecuador to invest a year of her life working with kids.

Teens today are very experiential. They need times to put their faith in action.

Teens today are very experiential. They need times to put their faith in action. Obviously, we can't all go with our kids to a foreign country to do mission work, but we can help them find the time to give them the opportunity to do hands-on ministry and learn that the call to Christ is the call to serve.

INTELLECTUAL CHANGE

"Who am I?" This seems to be the big question behind so much of adolescence. Of course, your teen is probably not using this exact phrase, but when you look at the various areas of their life issues, that is the question behind their actions.

The teen years are where kids move from concrete thinking to abstract. You can tell your elementary child what to do most of the time. With teens, they need dialog more than monolog. They need to be heard. Someone once said, "We must ask them rather than tell them." I'm not talking about discipline and boundaries. In this case, it's more about intellectual issues that relate to their identity.

One of the primary tasks of the teen years is to construct a personal identity. Most authorities agree that a majority of kids go through some type of an identity crisis while in their teens. They experiment with who they want to be, how they want to be perceived by others, and what life is about. Nick, for example, is into a certain style of dress and music, but over the summer he completely changes his musical tastes and look. He is just a young man trying to establish his identity. Adolescence is a time to redefine yourself. Today this is even more prevalent with social networking on the Internet. Some kids are forming their identities based on how they socialize online and how they are perceived through avenues like Facebook profiles, texting, and chat rooms.

Intellectually, your teen will change his opinion of you. When he was younger, you could most likely do little wrong. You were the most wonderful mom in the world or the smartest and strongest dad. But when kids reach their teen years, parents are no longer all-powerful and all-knowing. Some kids begin to view the world more realistically and feel let down by people who lack integrity. They see the plain old sinfulness of human nature. And as mentioned before, rebellion can be a natural part of the teen years. Family authority Les Parrott says, "Rebellion is a logical consequence of young people's attempts to resolve incongruent ideas and find authentic identity. Rebellion results from a desire to be unique while maintaining the security of sameness."[1]

The intellectual changes during adolescence are at least as big as the physical changes, but in some homes they go less noticed. It's such a time of discovery and experimentation that it can cause stress and turmoil for many young people, and they really don't know how to identify their issues. Again, they are in process. Chap Clark, author of many books and articles on teens and one of the foremost authorities in the world on adolescence, says this personal search toward adulthood involves the need for identity ("Who am I?"), autonomy ("Do my choices matter?"), and belonging ("Where do I fit?").[2] Knowing this information doesn't make the transition from childhood to adulthood any easier, but it does help parents understand the process and the needs. Kids mature in different stages and on a different time frame.

THE STAGES OF DEVELOPMENT

As kids shift their way of thinking and acting, so must parents. Parents have to shift their parenting style to keep up with what is going on in the life of their child. Just as we have looked at the different developmental changes that will take place, we also have to understand that even the age of adolescence has changed from just a few generations ago. In the times of our grandparents and great-grandparents, adolescence was much less complicated. It took about five years after puberty to make the transition to adulthood, and with much less stress.

Today, we can divide adolescent development into four stages, and at each stage parents have to regroup their parenting style. You will notice that in the following summary, ages overlap because kids develop at a different rate physically, socially, emotionally, spiritually, and intellectually.

Pre-Adolescence (ages 9 to 11)—This is a time of preparation for adolescence. Typically your kids are asking lots of questions, and you may even see the first physiological changes take place.

Early Adolescence (ages 11 to 14)—Puberty has set in. This time is characterized with lots of change and newness. Emotions are all over the place, and they are searching for their identity.

Mid-Adolescence (ages 14 to 18)—Experimentation is usually a major part of this period. You may see these kids a bit cynical about authority, and they can often be described as egocentric and self-absorbed. Friends are very influential. For some kids, by the later mid-adolescent years you are beginning to see the light of adulthood and healthy decisions.

Late Adolescence or Emerging Adulthood (ages 18 to mid-20s)—In other generations this was considered adulthood. Most people got married and perhaps were already starting a family. Today, parents are seeing their emerging adult children move back home and take longer to live independently. This gives rise to all kinds of complicated issues such as moral decisions and financial considerations. The issues that make up the adolescent years rarely are completed until the mid-twenties.

MISSION, MATE, MASTER

Someone once said, "Raising teenagers is like riding a roller coaster. Buckle your seat belt, hold on for dear life, and once the ride is over life will smooth out." When all is said and done, there are three key factors that you can speak into the life of your children during these critical years. This is not original with me, but something I picked up years ago as Cathy and I looked at one day launching our children into adulthood. It boils down to these three words: mission, mate, and Master.

As a parent, you can influence your child to find their mission or purpose in life. You can't do it for them, but you can sure help them find that thing that wakes them up each day with purpose. You definitely will not be able to choose a mate for them, as nice as that sounds on some days, but you can help them learn how to have healthy relationships. Whom they will one day marry will be a determining factor in how they will carry out their own legacy of life and faith. Most young people say they receive little instruction in how to build healthy relationships from their parents. Although they don't want lectures, they do want to have your input in this area. Last is Master. This is perhaps the most important role of a parent, to help their kids find a relationship with God that is real and vibrant and owned by them.

If you can offer your children input in these three areas of their lives—mission, mate, and Master—and they do make good decisions, then you have helped launch them toward a healthy adulthood and a legacy of faith that will continue from generation to generation.

FOUR

Creating a Media-Safe Home

People 24 and older use the Internet as a tool . . . but people under 24 use it as a way of life.

Roger Marsh

The actors, singers, and entertainers I know are emotional cripples. Really healthy people aren't in this business, let's face it.

Madonna

No parent has ever thought the world was perfectly safe for his or her children. We taught our children when they were young to look both ways before they cross the street and not to talk with strangers. We monitored the type of media they would view or at least we tried to keep up. However, in today's world it is almost impossible to have control over everything that is being sent to the eyes, minds, and brains of young people. So much of this generation's life is centered around media, and it is tempting them in every way.

Last week at a Purity Code conference at a church in Louisiana, the speaker took the high school boys into a room and asked, "How many of you have not viewed pornography on the Web?" Not one boy raised his hand. When I was young, boys might be able to sneak a peek at a dirty magazine every once in a while, but today the greatest distributor of porn is the cell phone, accessible twenty-four hours a day.

If anything is going to take down this generation of teenagers, it's going to be poor media choices, especially pornography.

From music, TV shows, and movies to teen magazines, video games, and, of course, the Internet, it all has an influence on teens today, and much of it is not good. I have said publicly many times that if anything is going to take down this generation of teenagers, it's going to be poor media choices, especially pornography. Most parents feel lost. Some feel hopeless. We complain to fellow parents, but it is time for us to fight the culture, quit whining, and one by one create media-safe homes where our kids will learn discernment regarding the vast amount of media that is being thrown at them.

One reason many of us feel somewhat helpless and even paralyzed by our kids' use of media is the learning curve it requires. After all, some of us still need our kids to fix the flashing numbers on our old VCRs and DVD players!

We can't afford to bury our heads in the sand when it comes to technology. We must become students of the culture and see how media is influencing our children. There is hope for those who persevere and try to create media-safe homes. At one time the "keep your kids in a bubble" approach might have worked, but that isn't going to happen today unless you move to a remote island, and with today's technology, that island may still have the same media choices!

HomeWord is the largest provider of Christian parenting seminars in the United States. Our topics range from "Understanding Your Teenager" to "Teaching Children Healthy Sexuality," but at the end of each seminar, when it's time for Q and A, the dominant questions are always focused on media: "Should I allow my kids on Facebook?" "How many hours a day should I let my kids play video games?" "What about music in the home?" "Where do we keep the computer?" The list goes on and on.

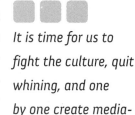

It is time for us to fight the culture, quit whining, and one by one create media-safe homes.

There is a story in the Bible about Joshua and Caleb and ten others sneaking into the Promised Land to scout it out and report back to Moses what they found (see Numbers 13). You could say they provided a majority report and a minority report. As they scouted the land, they found it to be "flowing with milk and honey." There was wonderful fruit and beautiful streams. The land was good. For people who had been wandering in the desert for so many years, it truly was the Promised Land. But there was one problem— it was inhabited by powerful giants who would not want the people of Israel to enter it. Ten leaders, the majority, advised Moses not to enter the Promised Land. "The land is beautiful with bountiful food, but giants live in the land." But when it came time for Joshua and Caleb to make their minority report, they basically said, "We agree. The land is wonderful and the people are like giants." But they added, "Let us immediately go into the land, for God will give us victory." Both groups saw the same things in the Promised Land. One group was paralyzed with fear, but Joshua and Caleb believed that with God's help they could inhabit the land flowing with milk and honey, and Moses went with the minority report.

My point is simple. As we take a look at the giant of media that is influencing the minds and lives of our children, either we can be paralyzed with fear or we can proactively take on the giant. Since we can't keep our children from all media, we will have to teach them to learn to discern what is influencing them.

TECHNOLOGY IS NEUTRAL, THE MEDIA IS NOT

Can I just admit upfront that I'm not very good with technology? I know how to turn on a computer (most of the time). I can usually get a DVD to play, but I still haven't figured out all the buttons on our fancy universal remote for the TV. I have been known to actually go over to the television and push the button on the front to turn it on or off, which drives my kids crazy. Still, I use technology. I love my iPhone, although I don't know about most of the apps and programs. I love the opportunity to use Twitter every day to a growing audience, and I am constantly amazed by the HomeWord Center for Youth and Family's Facebook page. The interaction and ability to communicate is incredible.

It is important for parents to understand that technology itself is neither good nor bad. Technology is neutral. Its value comes from how it is used. The same cell phone that could save a life or keep kids from danger can feed them gross pornographic images. MySpace can be a helpful tool your daughter's youth worker uses to invite her to a Bible study, but it can also be used by a sexual predator.

Parents, you don't need to become media experts—you just need to be aware of what's out there and how your kids are using the latest technology.[1] I've had parents tell me, "I just don't know how to use a computer," or "I'm too busy to keep up with all the media that my kids handle in a day." It may be overwhelming, but there is no excuse good enough to remain ignorant or in denial. When you decided to have a child, God entrusted to you the responsibility for his or her safety. Every child deserves their parent's best.

LISTEN, READ, AND WATCH

The easiest way to become a student of the culture and media that is influencing your teenagers is to *listen to what they listen to, read what they read, and watch what they watch.* Yes, this means you have the right to help choose what kind of music enters your home. Reading teen magazines, which are especially popular with girls, will give you an immediate handle on the youth culture. Sitting down to watch the television programs and movies your kids watch will enlighten you more than you may want. You also should check out Facebook and other social networking sites, video games, and other Web sites your kids tend to hang out on.

The best people to teach you about the influence of media are the teenagers you are closest to: your kids and your kids' friends. I keep a list of various media that I like to dialog about with kids, and I look for every opportunity to ask and learn. As I check out each type of media, I consider: How does this type of media influence my child (positively, negatively, neutrally)? How much time does my teen spend with this type of media each day? Each week? And what are the dangers of this type of media? Here's the list of media to be aware of:

- Social networking sites like Facebook and MySpace
- Texting
- Video gaming
- Computer gaming
- Movies
- Magazines
- DVDs, Blu-ray discs, and videos
- Music and music videos
- Internet
- Chat
- Blogs
- Television, broadcast and cable/satellite

Here's my advice:

1. *Evaluate everything you see and hear.* This takes a lot of work, but it's worth it. In our home, Cathy and I would divide and conquer. There was many a time when we had to draw the line with a certain music group or movie. When you evaluate, don't just put yourself in the bad-guy part. Tell your children what you like and why, and definitely help them learn to discern what they are putting into their minds.

I remember when one of my daughters brought home a new CD. On the surface it sounded okay to me, but

I just had a feeling about the band. So I went online and studied up on them. It was obvious they promoted drug use. Some in the band were married, but they clearly had no problem carrying on extramarital affairs. And one band member had been arrested for child pornography and relations with a minor. When I brought this to my daughter's attention, I took a deep breath and asked, "So what do you think?" She first talked about how she didn't listen to the words of the songs, but then she finally said, "They're gross. I'm not going to listen to them anymore." Okay, so she never thanked me for my investigative skills, but she made the decision to not listen to the group anymore, and I didn't have to pull the plug. As with many parenting decisions, you will just have to decide the battles worth fighting. Just know you won't always be thanked for evaluating your child's media. Still, it is your home, and you are responsible for what comes into your home.

2. *Examine your own behavior.* Too many parents want their children to view good healthy images and listen to clean music but aren't willing to discipline their own lives. If Dad watches raunchy movies and Mom reads *Cosmopolitan*, we should expect their children to want to do the same. Children see, children do. If Dad comes home from work and jumps on the computer for hours, the kids won't understand why they can't. I like to keep this verse in mind: "Everything is permissible for me, but not everything is beneficial. Everything is permissible for me, but I will not be mastered by anything" (1 Corinthians 6:12).

3. *Enter into dialog, not monolog.* Here is a great principle: Kids learn best when they talk, not when you talk. Anytime we can truly dialog about media use and influence, it is better than any lecture and sermon to our kids. Dialog tends to build them up—it honors them. You are saying, "I want to hear your point of view." Ultimately you may choose to disagree with them, but they will at least feel you were open-minded about their opinions. Lectures tend to close their spirit toward you, and after a while they shut you out or don't feel you are a safe person to try out new ideas with.

4. *Develop usage agreements for music, media, and the Internet.* As I discussed earlier, it is much more effective when young people have clearly expressed expectations. My suggestion is that you and your teen together come up with some type of an agreement on what is and what is not acceptable in your home. The agreements in the appendix (samples that Cathy and I used with our own children) may be helpful for you as you create your own agreements with your kids.

THE PARENT'S ROLE

Perhaps the two most prevalent approaches parents take toward media use don't work: ignoring the dangers and being too strict.

Some parents seemingly put their heads in the sand when it comes to their kids' media use. It takes a lot of work to help evaluate media, and kids are going to fight back about the choices. It's easy for a parent to get worn down and give up. Other parents say they are concerned about sex and violence coming into their home through various media outlets, but they do little about it, not even checking the rating systems or considering media-use agreements with their kids.

The other approach to media use that in my opinion doesn't work is trying to keep your teens in a bubble with too-tight restrictions. It might work during the younger years, but with teens, in general, boundaries that are too tight will cause them to rebel so much that they may run in the other direction.

The two most prevalent approaches parents take toward media use don't work: ignoring the dangers and being too strict.

So what's the answer? My input is that families should have boundaries and time limits for television, computer use, video gaming, texting, and any other media use. It's ultimately up to you to set and enforce those boundaries, but they will work best if you and your teen create them together. Remember, people support what they help create. I love the photo I took of one of my girls fast asleep in her bed with her head on the pillow and both hands curled around her cell phone at her cheek. Funny, but I didn't let it happen again. Obviously, boundaries will change as your kids move from pre-adolescence to emerging adulthood, but at every age kids need their parents' direction and guidance to help stay within healthy boundaries.

The difficult thing about all of this is that your kids won't always agree with you, and you will likely get old standby arguments like "I don't listen to the words" or "Everybody gets to watch that movie but me." Nevertheless, hold your ground, keep on top of their media use, and dialog as much as possible.

In our home, MTV was not an option. However, we did allow our kids to watch the MTV Video Music Awards show each year, as long as we watched it with them. It was a great opportunity to dialog as a family. We would almost always have a running commentary about the musicians and the songs. One year, a star was almost too intoxicated to accept her award. Another year, two of the world's mega female stars French kissed onstage. It was my opportunity to ask lifestyle-related questions rather than lecture. My girls already knew where I stood.

A few times Cathy and I took one of our kids to movies that "all her friends" were seeing. Two things helped. First, we made sure we didn't go to a theater where they would be seen with their parents! And second, but more important, we went out for fun food afterward and discussed the movie.

Helping teens discern the influence of media goes beyond focusing on the promiscuous acts in movies or TV shows or the raunchy songs on their iPods and radio stations. Media-related groups are doing extensive research on our kids, learning how to appeal to their basic needs, so it's important that we monitor our kids' attitudes and behaviors. In many cases, technology can isolate people from healthy relationships. My friend and colleague at Azusa Pacific University, Dr. David Peck, found his teenagers texting in the middle of the night. He now has a 9:00 p.m. rule, where the cell phones are all placed in their charging units and cannot be used without permission until 7:00 a.m. He also has worked it out with his cell carrier that there are only a few certain numbers the kids can call during school hours. Good idea.

Media can have such a powerful influence on our brains

that it is natural to begin to act out the drama of media. In my research of school killing sprees, I cannot find one murderer who had not been regularly viewing a strong dose of violence and listening to a style of music with violence. Pornography has the same effect. The stages of porn addiction move from viewing it to becoming addicted to increasing the number of views to being desensitized to it to acting it out in their mind and then in person. It's just too powerful of an effect on the human brain and emotions.

THE INTERNET, SOCIAL MEDIA, AND CELL PHONES

The Internet is here to stay, and its influence is only growing. Your teen will use the Internet more and more for social networking, entertainment, education, and overall communication. Facebook alone has a population the size of the fourth largest country in the world at four hundred million people and counting. One recent study found that one out of six American couples getting married today first met online.[2] Nearly all teens say that connecting online with a friend is the same as actually spending time with that person face-to-face. In fact, some students say their best friends are people they have never actually met except on the Internet.

When we were teenagers and we couldn't hang out face-to-face with our friends, the home phone was our only option. Most teens today would rather communicate through social networking Web sites, instant messaging, or cell phone text messaging. Is there any other parent besides me whose kids won't answer the phone but will immediately answer a text? They can multitask better via online methods, they can communicate quickly, and they can't be overheard by their parents.

Also, it's been suggested that due to parents' safety concerns in today's culture, many kids don't have the freedom to hang out with peers in settings that were common for us when we were teens. As a result, kids use social media to hang out "virtually" with their peers to socialize, chat, and share their thoughts.

When it comes to video, today's teens don't have to sit in front of a television for their entertainment. You-Tube, Hulu, and other social media sites make it possible for kids to watch what they want, when they want—on their computers and cell phones. On these sites they can watch, download, comment on, and share videos virally with others and even upload their own videos. More and more, teens are turning to social media to get their entertainment fix.

Like other forms of media, there are good and bad sides to the Internet. Your teen will use the Internet to write their school papers, receive inspiration, and stay in touch with their best friend, but it will also probably be where they see their first pornographic photo or video. With such a complex influence, it should be a top priority to talk with your kids about using the Internet and to establish some guidelines.

Here are some of my thoughts on handling the Internet, social media, and cell phones in your home.

Just a Click Away: Mature and Inappropriate Content

Although it is possible for kids to have a safe and positive experience using social media, understand that dangers lurk close by. It's important to know that kids are always a click or two away from content that you don't want them to view. As mentioned earlier, the cell phone is quickly becoming the number one distributor of pornography. It's not a stretch to say that if your kids are online, they will be exposed to porn (even if accessed unintentionally). The number one demographic for new users of Internet pornography is boys aged eleven to seventeen. If I were a teen today, I don't know if I could avoid the temptation. The dangers abound, and my fear is that many of today's

The number one demographic for new users of Internet pornography is boys aged eleven to seventeen.

teens will end up on the road to porn addiction. More about this in the next chapter, "Teaching the Purity Code."

Predators on the Prowl

Because of the veil of anonymity afforded by social media, some sexual predators pose as imposters, giving false information about their age and identity, including criminal histories, in order to gain the trust of "friends." They quite simply pretend to be someone they are not. However, you might be surprised to know that recent research indicates that most predators are actually up-front in engaging their victims online. They just search for kids who are willing to interact with them. In fact, of the kids who are victimized by sexual predators, most willingly meet with the predator knowing that they are interested in sex. Kids who engage in at-risk behaviors "offline" also turn out to be the most at-risk online.[3]

Experimenting

Many kids use social media to experiment with their social skills. The online atmosphere emboldens kids to communicate in ways they would not when in face-to-face conversation, or to engage in behaviors they typically would not. Sexual comments, "sexting" (taking seminude, nude, or other provocative photos for distribution via the Internet or cell phones, as well as receiving and forwarding them to others), criticisms, rants, and even cyberbullying are all commonly found in social media venues.

SET APPROPRIATE BOUNDARIES AND PROVIDE INTENTIONAL OVERSIGHT FOR SOCIAL MEDIA

- *Follow Web site rules and safety tips, and set privacy settings.* If you allow your kids to have access to social media, be sure to follow the rules and tips provided on specific Web sites. Additionally, when setting up a social networking account, be sure to access the security settings area to make sure your child's profile is private and to ensure only designated "friends" can access their profile. Also, as the parent in the home, you have every right to consistently check the history of Web sites your family has visited. If you don't know how to find the history, ask an experienced computer user for a one-minute lesson.

- *Keep a computer with online access out of their bedroom.* If your child is spending hours of unsupervised Internet access in the privacy of their bedroom, you are asking for trouble. If you already are allowing it, move it to a public place in the home. And don't expect to win a popularity contest with your teen on this one. Sometimes we just have to be the parent. You are not their best friend anyway. They already think you are old!

- *Set up a closed circle of online "friends."* On social networking Web sites, allow your kids to designate as friends only those people they know and of whom you approve. This will limit your kids to communicating with a specific, closed group of people.

- *Don't allow younger teens to add new online friends without your permission.* It's likely that over time, your children will want to add additional friends to their social networking profile. Your children might also receive requests from people they don't know to be added to their friend list. Set an expectation that no person can be added to the friend list without your permission.

- *Don't allow your kids to provide any personal information.* Don't allow kids to post any information that would make it easy for a stranger to find them, such as addresses, phone numbers, where they regularly hang out, where they work, and what time they get off work.

- *Don't allow kids to set up multiple profiles using multiple e-mail accounts.* From the beginning, set the expectation that your child is allowed only one account on a social networking Web site. Make sure your child understands they will be disciplined for violating this expectation.

- *Make it clear that you intend to be a "friend" and will regularly check your child's profile.* Your child will likely balk at this rule, as he or she will want their profile to be private, free from a parent's view. Don't give in. This will serve a couple of good purposes: ensuring that your children think through what to post on their profile before they do so, and giving you the opportunity to view the content that others post on the profile as well. Be sure to follow through. Visit their profile frequently, but resist the urge to make "mom" or "dad" comments on their site.

- *Have your kids agree to tell you if they receive any inappropriate or threatening messages.* The possibility exists that your child will receive uninvited, inappropriate, or threatening messages from others. Set the expectation that you need to know if this occurs so that you can deal with these messages. Tell your kids they will not get in trouble but you do want to know. There are just too many people on the Internet who are predators. The earlier you have this talk with your children the better. There is a fine line between meddling in a conversation and intervening, so use care in walking that fine line.

- *Set clear expectations about cell phone use.* These expectations should include all issues associated with today's cell phones, including texting, when it's okay to talk on their cell phone, and taking and distributing photos and videos. Tell your kids that if they receive inappropriate photographs from others, you expect them to notify you.

- *Set clear expectations about video Web sites.* Your kids need to know what you expect when it comes to visiting social media sites such as YouTube. Determine what types of video they can view and which ones they cannot. Understand that you probably won't be able to tell what videos they've watched, particularly if they access video through their phone or when they are away from home with their friends. If you set clear expectations, at least your kids will have to make a choice, knowing where you stand. Make sure they know that if they come across video of a pornographic nature, you're willing to talk it over with them.

- *Follow through with consistent discipline.* Kids need consistent discipline from their parents in order to both survive and thrive. That means clearly articulated limits, expectations, and consequences. If your kids violate your boundaries, it is key to follow through consistently with the agreed-upon consequences.

Not so many years ago, parents gave little thought about the need to create a media-safe home. Today, many rank it as the number one problem of raising their teens. Nevertheless, social media and all other forms of media are here to stay, and the issues will only get more complicated each year. How your child consumes media will impact her or his life for better or for worse. My parents had the benefit of monitoring the home phone, a few movie theaters around town, and the magazines in the house, but they

How your child consumes media will impact her or his life for better or for worse.

never worried about TV. Today's parent must be proactive on so many fronts and provide loving guidance and discipline, with good measures of patience and grace thrown in. In doing these things, you'll be helping your child grow into a mature and responsible adult who can use media in healthy ways.

FIVE

Teaching the Purity Code

I commit from this day on to live a life dedicated to sexual purity. Lord, help me to flee temptation but run to You. I will wait because I honor You.

Rebecca St. James

It just sort of happened. I wasn't planning on losing my virginity. He was cute and he told me he loved me. The next day he pretended like he didn't know me at school.

Jenny, age 15

Despite what the media report, many young people today *do* have the will and desire to live a life of sexual integrity and purity. Everybody is not "doing it." With the incredible amount of unhealthy influences from the world around them, your teen will have to go against the rising tide of culture and have the courage to stand for healthy sexuality. It won't be easy, but more and more studies are revealing that parental advice and role modeling is one of the major factors in helping young people make good decisions about their sexuality and relationships.

For many parents, the number one goal is to do everything possible to make sure their child stays pure until his or her wedding day. This is wonderful, but I believe we can and should do so much more for our children. We can help establish in them lasting sexual purity and integrity that extends throughout their lifetime.

The Bible speaks clearly about sexual purity, and for good reason. It is ultimately for the healthiness and well-being of our relationships. If your teen commits to a lifestyle of sexual integrity, it will help his or her marriage and family life in the long run. How many wives and husbands do you know who still carry "baggage" in their marriage from unwise decisions about sex and relationships in their younger years? For me, I'm afraid there are too many to count. As a person who speaks and writes on marriage issues, I am always amazed at how often sexuality is a key factor in a broken relationship.

One of my personal life ministry objectives is to help young people and their parents live by what I call the Purity Code. There were various types of purity codes in the Bible. Here is the commitment I am challenging young people and their families to make:

The Purity Code Pledge

In honor of God, my family, and my future spouse, I commit to sexual purity. **This involves:**

- Honoring God with my **body**
- Renewing my **mind** for the good
- Turning my **eyes** from worthless things
- Guarding my **heart** above all else

As you can see, choosing to live by the Purity Code is the opposite of what's promoted in today's hook-up society, where teens go from one sexual partner to the next. Your teen will need all the help and guidance possible.

THE TALK

Many parents ask me about the right age to have "the talk" with their kids. I always give the same response: "Never." The one-time birds-and-bees talk doesn't work. Whether it's about sex or any other topic important to our children, we need to create an open, trusting environment of healthy dialog, so when they need answers, they feel comfortable coming to us. As I've said before, lectures and preaching at your teen won't work well, especially if sexuality hasn't been discussed in your home before. The "don't have sex until you're married"

The one-time birds-and-bees talk doesn't work.

edict is definitely a good clear message, but it will not have as much weight on your teen's decision-making process as a series of conversations.

You might think your teen will tune out your advice about relationships and sex, but studies show that teenagers view their parents as the biggest influence on their sexual behavior. This means parents are more effective and important than friends, the media, educators, siblings, or even the church. Even so, young people today turn to the Internet for information on sex more than any other resource. I'm not sure you want to trust the Internet as a key provider of sex education for your children. I know I don't.

Talking about sexuality is hardly ever comfortable for a

parent or the child. Preteens and young teens are especially mortified by even the thought of a conversation with their parents. Yet delaying the conversation isn't good either, since recent studies show that almost 50 percent of parents have a conversation about sex *after* their kids have already had intercourse. With this in mind, have your conversations often and have them early.

From a developmental standpoint, the following is a simple way of looking at what to talk about and when. These thoughts are taken from the developmental research I did for my PURE FOUNDATIONS book series. I have included preteen information to give you an idea of the natural progression of sex-related discussions.

- *Ages 3 to 5*—Help kids learn about the parts of their bodies and the fact that one day they will grow up to be mommies and daddies. God created boys and God created girls. Their private areas are different from those of the opposite sex and their bodies are special.

- *Ages 6 to 9*—This is the age of curiosity. Answer their questions in an age-appropriate manner. At this age children are too young to have all the details of the sexual systems spelled out to them, but it is important for them to hear the basics about their bodies and even the bodies of the opposite sex. Because of the prevalence of sexual abuse of children, this is the age to teach them about appropriate and inappropriate touch. If anyone or anything makes them feel uneasy, they can feel comfortable coming to Mommy or Daddy to talk with them. Just because puberty hasn't kicked in at this age doesn't mean their sexuality is not an important part of their development.

- *Ages 10 to 14*—This is the best time to present the Purity Code to your children. Help them understand the importance of sexual integrity before they start dating. Talk with your children about how their bodies will change before they actually start to change. Then celebrate the changes. We have friends who have a private family party when their daughters begin having periods. No one in the family feels awkward about it because it has become a normal celebration and tradition to have this experience. The ages ten to fourteen are very critical to the development of healthy sexual values and building wholesome relationships. Look at this as a time of prevention and training in healthy relationships with the opposite sex.

- *Ages 14 and up*—By age fourteen, feel free to talk about anything and everything. The media is shouting a much different set of values than those you want your kids to live by. Many music, movie, and athletic stars are not the role models we want our kids following; however, because of the silence of the family on this subject, these people become the role models who influence our children. If you haven't talked about oral sex, masturbation, and other important but often-difficult issues, know that others will gladly have those conversations with your kids from a different worldview than yours. If you haven't talked with your kids about sex, it's not too late. Just dive in and start the process. There are excellent resources out there to help you. But don't wait. I'm reminded of a cartoon I read in the newspaper where a father and his teenage son are sitting in a fishing boat in the middle of a lake. The son angrily says to his dad, "You got me out here just so you could have the sex talk with me?" With a sheepish look, the dad says,

"Don't get mad, Jeremy. I just thought this might be an opportunity for us to have a frank Q and A session about sex." Jeremy replies, "Okay, fine. I'm sorry for yelling at you. Now, Dad, what did you want to know?" Obviously, that's not how it's supposed to work.

PORNOGRAPHY: COULD IT TAKE DOWN OUR CULTURE?

Pornography is wreaking havoc on the minds and hearts of young people today. It's definitely not a feel-good parenting topic, but it must be addressed and it must be discussed with your teen. It is possible you made it through the teen years without viewing pornography. That is probably not the case with your child. The Internet and cell phones have brought porn up close and personal into the life of every young person in America, even if viewed by accident. The average age someone first sees porn today is before the age of twelve.

The problem with porn is that our minds take a picture of everything we view, which means countless kids have pornographic images forever embedded in their minds. These kids will tend to struggle with viewing the opposite sex as sex objects and worse. Sex becomes nothing but a sex act, without the physical and emotional intimacy ordained by God since creation itself.

Countless kids have pornographic images forever embedded in their minds.

Pornography is extremely addicting for many people. Once they have viewed porn, it escalates in their lives. If you teach your kids the Purity Code and the four important biblical standards behind the code, it doesn't leave room for porn. Honoring God with your body, renewing your mind for the good, turning your eyes from worthless things, and guarding your heart simply can't be done with regular viewing of pornography. Even so, we parents need to be proactive about helping our kids learn about the dangers of pornography and its stages of addiction:

1. *Viewing pornography.* Most kids will view pornography. Many will feel ashamed or think it is dirty but at the same time find it intriguing and mysterious. The images often draw them back to view more porn and move them toward addiction. Pornography is so prevalent that when Canadian researchers recently wanted to compare men in their twenties who had never been exposed to pornography with regular viewers of pornography, the project stumbled at the first hurdle because they failed to find a single man who had not viewed porn.[1]

2. *Addiction.* Take the brain's power to store images and replay them and add it to the curiosity and sexual nature of most teens, and you can understand how easy it is for young people to become addicted to porn and want to return again and again to images that stimulate them.

3. *Escalation.* As a person becomes addicted to porn, their brain craves the stimulation, and much like alcoholism or gambling addictions, there is a desire to view it more often. One young man said, "I'm hungry for porn. In fact, I would rather view pornography than eat."

4. *Desensitization.* Along with addiction and escalation, the mind now becomes desensitized to what at first might have even bothered the person. What was gross

three months ago or even three weeks ago is now appealing. As with any type of addiction, the mind and body crave more and look for a stronger high, which in the case of porn can be experiences that are more and more vile, violent, and frankly, gross.

5. *Acting out.* In the advanced stages of porn addiction, people act out the experiences in their mind, sometimes write about them in Internet chat rooms, and eventually want to act out with another person what they have seen.

Sexual addiction is growing among young people, and pornography is the main culprit. This is why it is so important to have ongoing conversations with our children about sexual purity and integrity—with the goal that they will be comfortable talking about what they might have seen and seek help. Accountability is one of the key ways to overcome porn addiction. Whether it is with porn or another sensitive subject, it is usually difficult for a parent to be their child's accountability partner. But do encourage your kids to have accountability relationships with both peers and trusted adults.

Our family chose to have very active godparents, other trusted adults, and youth group leaders in our life whom our kids could freely talk to, without everything being reported back to us. Involvement with porn or other sexual sins is one of the hardest things to admit to someone else, but regular accountability is what can keep someone from moving back into the addiction. Of course, the safest spot is for your kids to never get involved in the first place. For this to happen, have age-appropriate discussions with your teen and keep tight reins on computer privacy.

SEXTING

Many topics about sexuality can be uncomfortable to talk about, yet it's important for parents to be aware of them and, yes, even dialog with their teens about them. Ranking right up there with porn is "sexting." As mentioned earlier, sexting is sharing sexually explicit nude or seminude photos or videos through the texting device of a phone. If you think your kids have never heard of sexting, think again. The Associated Press reported a full 30 percent of young people have been involved in some form of sexting. One young man in California sent his girlfriend nude photos of himself so she would do the same thing in return. When he got her nude photo, he thought it would be "funny" to send it on to a friend of his at school. The girl was mortified and the law saw no humor in the situation. The young man was arrested for distributing child porn.

It is important to have conversations with your teens about sexting and, because you most likely pay for their cell phone, to let them know you have the right to check it from time to time.

ORAL SEX AND YOUNG PEOPLE

I can't even imagine seeing a section on oral sex in parenting books when I was younger. Today, oral sex is so prevalent it must be talked about to understand the hook-up culture in which our teens live. According to a recent *Journal for Adolescent Health* article, in a federal survey of more than 2,200 males and females aged fifteen to nineteen, more than half reported having had oral sex. Those who described themselves as virgins were far less likely to say they had tried oral sex than those who had had intercourse.[2] An earlier survey of adolescents found that half of them had engaged in oral sex at least once.[3] Is this alarming? You bet it is.

The Christian middle school near us had to bring in someone to talk with the kids about oral sex. Although these young teens had decided not to have sexual intercourse before marriage, they were having OS parties. The OS stood for oral sex. The kids justified their actions because it "wasn't really sex." The Centers for Disease Control (CDC) is this country's health organization, and even the CDC is concerned about this issue, as well as the epidemic of sexually transmitted diseases among teens. If this information is new to you, or you don't know what to say to your kids about issues like these topics, there are excellent resources that will help you gain information to pass along to your kids. As Dorothy said in *The Wizard of Oz*, "Toto . . . we're not in Kansas anymore."

Today, oral sex is so prevalent it must be talked about.

MEDIA

Chapter 4, "Creating a Media-Safe Home," covered lots of ground about sexuality and the media. Still, to help your children live by the Purity Code, know this: *Exposure to sexual media content may prompt teen sex.* According to one study, twelve- to fourteen-year-olds exposed to sexual content in movies, music, magazines, TV, and the Internet were 2.2 times more likely to have had sexual intercourse when re-interviewed two years later than their peers who had a lighter sexual media diet.[4] There is no doubt that kids who view explicit sexuality on media are influenced toward that kind of behavior. With so much sexual content in the media, there are endless opportunities to bring about parent-teen communication, as long as we keep it in a dialog format. If a parent only rants and raves about the terrible stuff on TV, then kids are not going to be as open to discussion and listening to their parent. Try to keep it a two-way conversation.

WHAT ABOUT DATING?

It sure was easier with our children when boys were yucky and girls had cooties. As the teen years progress, the words *yucky* and *cooties* are replaced with *hotties*!

It is a natural and even healthy progression for teens to have a growing interest in the opposite sex. For some, it starts early, even before adolescence. For others, it doesn't happen until later. One of our daughters was five when she started talking about liking certain boys. She would tell us who her latest boyfriend was and who she was going to marry. Another daughter was closer to her girlfriends and didn't have a serious boyfriend crush until college.

Part of helping our kids grow up to be responsible adults is to lead them in a healthy view of the opposite sex. I emphasize to young people that they are called to have a *radical respect* of the opposite sex. I love Paul's advice to the Romans: "Outdo one another in showing honor" (Romans 12:10).

Kids today are dating at alarmingly young ages. It is good for children to have positive experiences relating to the opposite sex, but to allow dating at ages twelve, thirteen, or fourteen worries me, and here's why. According to one study, of the kids who were in exclusive dating relationships at age twelve, 91 percent had had sexual intercourse before finishing high school. For the kids who waited until age sixteen to date exclusively, that percentage went down to 20 percent.

There are two types of dates—inclusive and exclusive. Inclusive is where a few boys and girls spend time together in a non-physical, non-romantic experience. Exclusive dating involves a boy and a girl spending time together alone. With the right supervision, inclusive dating is how teens learn best to relate to the opposite sex. However, exclusive dating at younger ages, even if it is not a sexual relationship, sometimes revs up the engines too soon and leads the way toward early sexualization. Kids make sexual decisions based on emotional involvement that exceeds their maturity levels. I have observed many really good kids at too early of an age get way over their heads and hearts in exclusive relationships.

I have two distinct memories of knowing I needed to confront my daughters about dating issues. Rebecca was about fourteen and madly in love with a boy. I knew it was puppy love, but puppy love is real to puppies! The calls and meetings were getting out of hand. She got to be a bit secretive about the relationship, and I noticed she was breaking some of our established expectations. I took her out to her favorite Chinese restaurant and replayed a conversation I had rehearsed about not letting her spend time with this boy except during school. We talked about some of the circumstances and her broken promises. She took it like I thought she would. She cried over her orange peel chicken and won ton soup. If I remember her words correctly, she declared, "You are ruining my life!" It was hard to hold my ground, but I did. I remember playing the what-if game in my head. *What if she rebels? What if she hates me for the rest of her life?* Recently we were laughing about the experience, and Rebecca couldn't even remember the boy's name. (I do. It was Ryan!)

With Christy, I remember her leaving me in the middle of a Subway sandwich shop after I told her what I thought of her relationship with a boy. It took her a day to cool down and at least listen to what I had to say. Today she agrees with my opinion, but it took a while. I wasn't running a popularity contest but helping her learn about relationships. I have found that as long as I place more deposits in the lives of my kids, then periodically I can afford to take a withdrawal.

USING THE GIFT OF SEXUALITY AS GOD INTENDED

During the writing of this book, I was invited to speak at a large church in Monroe, Louisiana, for a church-sponsored Purity Code weekend. It was a privilege to help the parents learn how to teach their kids healthy sexuality and to preach at the services. But for me, the most inspiring part of the weekend occurred when someone else was speaking.

After dinner on Saturday, my hosts asked if I wanted to go back to the church and see a youth evangelist from South Carolina challenge the students to live by the Purity Code. I was tired from speaking Friday night and all day Saturday, but I said yes. I was curious to see how someone I didn't know would use the material I had written to help kids make one of the most important decisions of their lives—to live with sexual purity. My goal is to have one million teens make a commitment to follow the Purity Code, and one of their first steps is signing a HomeWord Purity Code pledge card. The evangelist told me that earlier that day, in a break-out session attended by more than one hundred boys, all of them said they had seen pornography at some point in their young lives. The words *all of them* hit me hard.

That evening, after a time of worship (I love watching kids worship God), the evangelist went through the Purity Code with the two hundred fifty or so teens. It was a simple yet profound message. He invited them to fill out a pledge card and pray, but *only* if they felt led to do so, and not because of peer pressure. As the worship band started a new song, the majority of the kids got up out of their chairs and signed those commitment cards— many on their knees and some with tears in their eyes. Students prayed with each other and with adults. I'm sure some needed to deal with past issues of sexual abuse or promiscuity. The youth room was transformed into a holy sanctuary of love and honor to God.

The kids didn't have any idea that a certain nerdy bald guy in the back was crying his eyes out with joy. The next day I was introduced to the group, and I told them how they had inspired me and made me proud. Later that evening in the church service, the students had a special ceremony with their parents to celebrate their commitment to God and the Purity Code. I wasn't able to be there, but parents later told me it was a highlight for their family.

If not you, who will teach your kids about sex?

Special programs at church can definitely help to spark good conversations with your kids, but they are not necessary. Part of the parenting job description is to develop open and honest dialog with your kids about anything and everything, but especially about sexuality and relationships. If not you, who will teach your kids about sex? The Internet? Pop stars like Madonna? Teachers with a different moral compass?

Don't let someone else be the most influential person in your child's life.

Remember, we don't teach our children to live by the Purity Code just to keep them away from sex before marriage. That's too low of a goal. Rather, it is to help them make wise decisions, to help them enter their marriage with less baggage, and to build upon the strong discipline of fidelity and faithfulness it takes to choose sexual purity rather than society's hook-up lifestyle. The result is that kids begin to understand that their sexuality is a gift from God and is intended to honor Him.

SIX

Communication Is Key

Nobody will listen to you unless they sense that you like them.

Donald Miller

Prize above all else those who love you and wish you well.

Alexandr Solzhenitsyn

The deepest principle in the human nature is the craving to be appreciated.

William James

Most teenagers can keep you mad at them 24/7/365. Not only is it a time when they are causing you newfound worries and concerns, but their communication with you rapidly deteriorates to one-syllable answers, closed doors, and a desire to keep you at a distance. What is amazing is that teens can text their friends a hundred times a day and talk on the phone for hours about nothing, but you often can't get more than a "fine" out of them when you ask about their day. If younger children are indeed like dogs and teens are like cats, a friend described his kids' attitudes this way: "To a dog you are family, and to a cat you are staff!"

When I speak at parenting conferences, I usually ask parents how many moms and dads are enjoying good communication with their teenagers. About 5 percent raise their hands. So if you are having trouble communicating with your teen, apparently you are in the vast majority. When I ask the parents if they communicated well with their parents when they were teens, or even liked their parents during those years, about 5 percent again raise their hands. It doesn't change the challenge you face or the possible hurt, but I hope it's good to know you aren't alone.

ATMOSPHERE IS EVERYTHING

When it comes to communication advice in many books about raising teens, the emphasis seems to be on technique and tips. I will give you some of those later in this chapter, but I personally don't think they are as important as setting a positive tone and atmosphere around the home. No home environment is perfect, and if you never experience conflict with your teens, something might not be right. However, you can often distinguish a healthy home atmosphere from an unhealthy one by the amount of chaos happening around you on most days. Here is the deal: I don't think we should solely blame our kids for chaos in the home. Their "job" as teenagers is bound to cause some chaos and conflict. They are experimenting with behaviors, challenging authority, and generally doing things to mess up any positive atmosphere around them. Your job in the home is to set a tone and atmosphere that is more conducive to a *better* environment for the family. Remember, I didn't say that raising great teens would be easy!

If your family is living at too fast of a pace, or if your own life is filled with chaos and conflict, don't expect your teens to set a positive atmosphere in your home. And don't expect communication to be all that good either. It's back to the intentional parenting of teens by staying calm, working a plan, and getting as emotionally healthy as you possibly can.

What is the atmosphere like in your home? If it needs some work, no problem. As I said, you are in good company with the majority of parents of teens. To set a better atmosphere you will need to be intentional, and you will sometimes have to decide when certain behaviors and choices are just not worth a battle. If your children see you as constantly nagging or criticizing them, don't expect them to enjoy hanging around with you. *Children need more models of healthy behavior than criticism.* Maya Angelou said it this way, "If you have only one smile in you, give it to the people you love. Don't be surly at home, then go out in the street and start grinning 'Good morning' at total strangers."[1] True, it is often easier to be kind and warm to someone we don't live with. But dropping your guard and allowing yourself to be negative most of the time with your kids isn't going to invite them to communicate with you.

RUTHLESSLY ELIMINATE STRESS

Families need more calm and less stress. The breathless pace of life is tearing at the core of family communication. When a family is overcommitted, it quickly becomes under connected. There will always be some stress in a family. It's the norm. But much stress can be removed with firm choices and more control of a runaway schedule. It's an old saying, but we have to learn not to prioritize our schedule but rather to schedule our priorities.

When a family is overcommitted, it quickly becomes under connected.

I keep a prayer displayed in my office that helps keep me centered on what's important. It's titled "Slow Me Down, Lord":

> Slow me down, Lord! Ease the pounding of my heart by the quieting of my mind. Steady my hurried pace with a vision of the eternal reach of time. Give me amid the confusion of the day, the calmness of the everlasting hills. Break the tensions of my nerves and muscles with the soothing music of the singing streams that live in my memory. Teach me the art of taking minute vacations—of slowing down to look at a flower, to chat with a friend, to pat a dog, to smile at a child, to read a few lines from a good book. Slow me down, Lord, and inspire me to send my roots deep into the soil of life's enduring values, that I may grow toward my greater destiny. Remind me each day that the race is not always to the swift; that there is more to life than increasing its speed. Let me look upward to the towering oak and know that it grew great and strong because it grew slowly and well.[2]

What practical steps can you take to create a calmer home atmosphere? Maybe it's as simple as turning down the volume on the TV or music. Or just turning it completely off. It's definitely doing things to take the rush and constant urgency out of each day. Do you have scheduled times in the week for family connection? Do you eat most of your evening meals together without it being a big chaotic rush? Are you renewing your spirit on a daily basis? Do you have time to renew your body on a regular basis with enough rest, plenty of exercise, and a healthy diet?

If there is a yearning within you to communicate more effectively with your family, there are plenty of things you can do to lead the way. I am not being idealistic and I am not saying it is easy, but quality communication time will not happen in the midst of chaos.

ARE WE HAVING FUN YET?

Milton Berle, the great comedian of another period, said, "Laughter is an instant vacation." Long before that, King Solomon shared these wise words: "A cheerful heart is good medicine, but a broken spirit saps a person's strength" (Proverbs 17:22 NLT). Much of the poor communication in families has little to do with communication technique and much to do with the nature of a busy lifestyle. Families are spending less time playing together in this generation than any generation before. Families need to laugh and play together. Sharing fun times is one of the best things for family togetherness and good communication. When a family laughs and plays together, it is emotionally nourishing.

How is your family's laughter quotient? As kids become teenagers, families have to be much more proactive and intentional about playing together. Play deprivation in families can easily shut down togetherness and communication and instead bring on hostility and negativity. Play and laughter are a release. Nothing turns off a teenager quicker than adults who have lost their sense of humor. It is often overlooked in parenting literature, but there is no doubt that healthy families are usually characterized by an abundance of laughter. Adolescent expert Wayne Rice says, "If laughter comes easily for your family, then getting through tough times will come a lot easier also. Wise parents aren't afraid to let their hair down once in a while and have fun with their kids whenever they can."[3]

My youngest daughter, Heidi, is the person who brings fun to our home most often. Her smiles and positive attitude about life bring a smile to the rest of us more intense members of the Burns household. In this last year I went through treatment for prostate cancer. It was Heidi who came to visit me from college with a balloon that said, "The Party Is Here!" It was exactly what I needed. I had plenty of support, mushy cards, and prayers. I also needed a good laugh, and she provided it. Playing and laughing together may open up the communication lines better than anything else.

A.W.E.

Lately I haven't been able to write a marriage or parenting book without bringing up the acrostic A.W.E. It stands for affection, warmth, and encouragement. This is really more of a testimony of my own thoughts on communication with my family and wife than anything else.

Many people resort to shame-based parenting to try moving their teenagers to action and obedience. If your parents used that style on you, I'm guessing it didn't work. It still won't. On the other hand, family relationships showing lots of *affection*, filling the home with an atmosphere of *warmth*, and providing tons of *encouragement* to the kids does wonders for effective communication. I learned how important it was to communicate with A.W.E. just as my children were entering the treacherous teenage years. I will say it again, but having all girls, we had our share of emotion and drama. Come to think of it, we still do! What I had to learn was to not always react to the emotion of the moment but be intentional about showering my daughters with A.W.E.

Being generous with appropriate affection brings security to kids. Girls crave healthy affection from their fathers. Boys need affection too. Sometimes it's a hug and other times it's wrestling. If you have a hard time offering affection to your teens because of their awkward stage or your own family history, I have three words for you: Get over it. Kids need affection from their parents in their teen years as much as in their younger years. If they don't get it from home, they will often look for it from others, even if it is inappropriate affection. The very last words my mother said to me before she died were "I love you, and I'm proud of you." I carry that gift of affection with me at all times. I try to say those words to my kids all the time.

Being generous with appropriate affection brings security to kids.

As you know, there is no such thing as a home without conflict, but communication is best when the home has a tone and atmosphere of warmth. We live near the Pacific Ocean, and sometimes on a chilly evening we still like to go down to the beach and light a bonfire. Its warmth always draws us closer. Genuine warmth in the relational atmosphere in the home will do the same thing.

It takes discipline to put aside our own issues and bring warmth to the relationship with your teen. Just today I had four major things to discuss with my daughter. I asked her out for breakfast, but I could tell she wasn't in the mood to talk as seriously as I wanted to talk. I kept my list in my pocket and mainly just listened to her "stuff." That's hard to do for a dad who almost always has an agenda. But that breakfast was not the time. So after having a fun meal with lots of laughter, I said, "I'd like to check in with you on a few things sometime in the next twenty-four hours," and we set a time for later in the day. In this case, what needed to be said could be dealt with seven hours later, and the warmth created at breakfast would serve to help the foundation of conversation later. It's the pain of discipline or the pain of regret. In communication if we discipline with warmth, we won't have as many regrets with the outcome or the timing.

Encouragement is food for our souls. Charles Schwab once said, "I have yet to find the man, however great or exalted in his station, who did not do better work and put forth greater effort under a spirit of approval than he would ever do under a spirit of criticism." Constant criticism of a teen, even if a bit justified, will cause them to run from you. Parents who nag a lot and constantly criticize close their child's spirit. I'm convinced that most kids who come from critical homes will try to be more deceptive than in homes of grace and affirmation. They so badly want to avoid criticism that they will try to lie their way out of every predicament.

With a teenager you can almost always find the bad if you look for it. But the opposite is true too. Look for the good, and don't be afraid to give your kids the gift of encouragement. If you look for the best in people, you will get the best in return.

ATTITUDE IS EVERYTHING

When it comes to good and healthy communication, attitude is everything. I tell parents all the time, "You have to take the lead with your attitude. You can't expect your teens to go someplace with their attitude that you haven't gone yourself." Emotionally unhealthy parents produce emotionally unhealthy kids. When the Bible talks about inheriting the sins of previous generations to the third and fourth generation, I think it relates to family attitudes as well. If you were raised in an environment of put-downs, pessimism, and disapproval, you will probably have to work harder than others not to repeat the pattern of negativity or a poor attitude with your children. But with focus and work, you absolutely can be the transitional generation and improve your family's pattern of communication.

I tell parents all the time, "You have to take the lead with your attitude."

Optimists choose action over wallowing in a communication quagmire. An optimist learns that what happens to him or her doesn't count as much as how they react. I have had to share with my kids that their circumstances may not ever change, but their attitude can, which makes all the difference in the world. Science tells us that optimists end up healthier with a more successful life and with much more success in relationships. Pessimism breeds poor decisions and poor relationships. A child in a home that communicates more pessimism will tend to run toward anything that will medicate her pain. Sometimes pessimism breeds chaos and chaos breeds misbehavior. You can't mentor and disciple your children if they live under your spirit of disapproval all the time.

When conflict and chaos arise in the home, it is easy to move directly toward being negative. However, if the home places an emphasis on having an attitude of thankfulness, it really changes the tone and mindset, even if it doesn't change the circumstance. I love what someone once taught me: "If the only prayer you ever prayed was 'Thank you,' that would be enough." For most self-absorbed teenagers, gratitude must be a learned trait. Our family periodically practices what we call *thank therapy*. We make a list of at least twenty reasons why we are thankful and then share them with each other. It never fails to change our attitudes and improve how we communicate.

RELAX!

For all the talk about teens with attitudes, we parents might need greater attitude adjustments. When Mom or Dad tries to own all the problems of the teen or gets too anxious about his or her parenting, it's the child who often becomes anxious, and a cycle of poor communication begins. Dr. Dave Stoop told me on a HomeWord radio program that "neither the parent nor the child benefit from anxiety. In fact, parental anxiety makes life very difficult for the parent and the child, since the child responds to the anxiety of the parents with even more severe anxiety, and then their anxieties aggravate each other." Of course, this goes back again to a major theme of this book, that parents of teens must get as emotionally healthy as possible. When we are relaxed as parents, we will make better decisions in the midst of tension and have the reserves to work on any issue our teen throws at us.

DEALING WITH ANGER

A woman was talking to me about her child who was giving her an especially challenging time, and she asked, "How do I deal with the anger issue?" I smiled. "Your anger or your daughter's anger?" She paused a moment, then said, "My daughter's, but come to think of it, I'm angry at her much of the time too."

It's always best not to discipline or say things in anger. Just bite your tongue. Most of the regrets I have in life come from what I have said in anger. People deal with anger in many ways. I'm not a yeller, though I am a stuffer. Other people rage and scream. Regardless of how we vent our anger, it's important to deal with it. Your kids will learn most how to deal with their frustrations and anger as they watch you. Unfortunately, in anger, it's easy to say hurtful things. We also end up saying silly things occasionally, like the time my father shouted at me when I was about nine years old, "Do you want a spanking?" Even then I wanted to reply sarcastically, "I was thinking about going out to play, but now that you mention it, maybe a spanking would be a good idea." No, when emotions are heated, it's always best to get your head in a better place and not say anything in anger.

If you do say or do something wrong, there is great power in immediately admitting it and telling your teen you are sorry. An apology is not a sign of weakness; it is a sign of strength and healthy authority. Saying you are sorry is one of the best ways you can model healthy communication for your teen. I remember hearing somebody say, "An apology is the superglue of life! It can repair just about anything." Your teen has long known you are not the perfect parent they thought you were when they were five years old. So just agree with them and apologize.

Saying you are sorry is one of the best ways you can model healthy communication for your teen.

In a HomeWord radio interview I had with the outstanding author and speaker Gary Chapman, he talked about five successful ways to apologize. I have used all five with my wife and kids.

1. *Expressing regret.* This is the emotional component of an apology, the "I'm sorry." This is admitting that you've hurt someone and that you are hurting because you've caused him or her pain.

2. *Accepting responsibility.* This step is often overlooked in today's families, but it is a necessary one for a successful apology. Regardless of whether the hurt was intentional or unintentional, accepting responsibility means saying, "I was wrong. It was my fault."

3. *Making restitution.* This language takes the apology to another level by asking, "What can I do to make this wrong right?" It demonstrates a willingness to take action to bring healing to the relationship.

4. *Repentance.* This step acknowledges your sentiment that you don't want the offense to happen again, and that you will take all the necessary steps within your power to see that it does not reoccur. This requires both a plan and implementation of the plan to keep the offense from happening again.

5. *Requesting forgiveness.* Asking, "Will you forgive me for what I've done to hurt you?" reflects the spiritual nature of your offense. The person you've hurt may choose not to forgive you. You can't force forgiveness, but asking for it is the right thing to do (see Matthew 5:23–24). Whether the person chooses to forgive is his or her responsibility, not yours.

HANDLING CONFLICT

When you put the words *teenager* and *communication* together, they often equal conflict. Since most of us were never taught how to handle conflict, we tend to do it wrong. We react poorly, or try to avoid conflict altogether. Henry Ford said, "Most people spend more time and energy going around problems than in trying to solve them." This sure seems to be true for parents of teens. We run from conflict for several reasons, but all conflict is not bad. I love these wise words I heard someone say: "When we long for a life without difficulties, remind us that oaks grow strong in contrary winds and diamonds are made under pressure."

There is a positive path through conflict and a negative path. The negative route is the path of protection—we are more interested in protecting ourselves from pain and fear. We are closed and defensive, which leads to power struggles, pain, distance, deadness in the relationship, and lack of intimacy. The positive route through conflict is the path of growth, and it is by far the healthiest for everyone involved. There is an intent to grow and learn. We do not react defensively. We try to understand ourselves and the other person better. We do not necessarily see criticism as an insult to our self-esteem.

As parents we have to assume personal responsibility for our feelings, behaviors, and even our consequences. It's more of a process of exploration, and the result of this path is resolution of the conflict and relationship growth. Most often there is a sense of well-being and love. The positive path takes more work and discipline, but the results are much better, and typically your children will learn how to deal with conflict more positively. So take the lead and make generational changes in how your family communicates.

COMMUNICATION TIPS

- *Make mealtime family time.* My good friend David Lynn is a counselor in Tucson, Arizona, and coined the phrase "Make mealtime family time." He has helped to bring to light overwhelming research showing that teenagers who dine regularly at home with their families are more satisfied with life. They are better students, are less likely to be sexually promiscuous, and tend to be much less involved with drug and alcohol abuse. Hectic schedules make dining together difficult, but the rewards make this a family tradition to cherish. A family I know, the Terrys, builds on this tradition every Monday night with an "ice cream run." I think the emphasis is more on the ice cream than the "run" part. It apparently works, though. You might think the novelty would wear off, but they tell me the family has gone out for ice cream for years and the teenagers never seem to have other things going on Monday nights.

- *Make bedtime communication time.* I found that one of the best times to have good communication with my teens was their bedtime. This was a carryover from their younger years when we tucked them into bed and said a prayer. When the teens were in bed but not asleep, I found them more in tune with talking about their day or their problems or whatever was on their mind. The relaxed atmosphere seems to work well for good communication. This is the type of communication that is foundational for the other times when you have to have a more difficult conversation. Try not to have those tougher conversations always at the same time or in the same place.

- *Have parent-child dates or hangout times.* By the time kids are teenagers, they are very focused on their friends and peers. They literally are becoming individuals away from Mom and Dad, but most are willing to do something fun with their parents; they still like to eat or shop. My habit was to have a monthly date with each of my children. They got to pick the experience, within financial reason. For them it mainly had to do with food. Another friend of mine took each of his two sons to breakfast every week. They didn't seem to mind getting up a bit earlier than usual before school. These days, his sons are married but live in the same area, and the weekly breakfast is still happening.

- *Walk around the block.* My good friend John Townsend, author and speaker extraordinaire, regularly took his sons on a walk around the block. At first they would complain, he said, but about the second time around the block "the floodgates of communication would open." Do whatever it takes to keep the communication lines open with your kids.

- *Listen more, talk less.* A great deal of communication is listening. Listening is the language of love. We parents can have a difficult time really listening to our children. It often seems easier to lecture and scold, but the results aren't the same as with listening. I've learned that sometimes my kids just want to talk and they really don't want me to share my opinion. I had to learn to quit answering all their questions . . . before they asked them! For older teens, it might help if you ask their permission to share your opinion, saying something like, "Would you mind if I shared with you my perspective?" This gives them a feeling that you really care for them. Even when it comes to conflict, a principle John Rosemond shared has the best results: "The fewer words a parent uses, the more authoritative the parent sounds. The fewer words a parent uses, the clearer the instruction."[4]

CONNECTION AND PRESENCE

If your teenager is making it clear he or she wants you to stay out of their life, your presence still matters. Part of your job is communicating care and connection in a way that means something to them. Dads who say they are showing their love by working sixty hours a week and seldom connecting with their kids are just wrong. Moms who constantly say, "Look at all I do for you" but don't show care and connection with the love language of their child are doing it wrong. Your presence matters. Kids who have a strong sense of connection to their parents are less likely to indulge in at-risk behaviors. When we think of communication with our teens, it really is about relationship more than rules. As so many family experts say, "Rules without relationship equals rebellion."

I have kept the following words, written by an unknown author, close to my heart. They take me back to the true priorities for communicating with my family.

Four Things You Can't Recover

The stone . . . after the throw
The word . . . after it is said
The occasion . . . after it is missed
The time . . . after it is gone.

A good reminder for us all.

SEVEN

The Spiritual Life of a Teenager

You can't really pass on to your children something that
you yourself don't have. . . . If you are doing all you can
to stay close to God, your kids will be much more likely
to want to do the same.

Wayne Rice

I grew up in the shadows of Disneyland. This magical place
of joy and creativity seemed to play a central part in many
of my friend's lives. Some of our parents worked there, we
had our birthday and graduation parties there, and as we
became teens, many of us took jobs at the original "magic
kingdom." (Some friends' jobs were glamorous, but others,
like me, worked as super duper pooper scoopers after the
horses in the parades!) When I was a child, the incredible
Matterhorn roller coaster was my favorite. I never tired of
riding it over and over again, up and down. Just recently
my wife and I went back to Disneyland, and the first ride
she wanted to go on was the roller coaster. It brought back

great memories. The only problem was, halfway through the ride I thought I was going to vomit! I like calmer rides these days, the kind that don't make my insides feel like they are churning all around.

The spiritual life of most teenagers is much more like a roller coaster than a calm and gentle ride. As teens move from dependence toward independence, they naturally begin to explore and even question their spiritual belief system. I have talked with what seems like hundreds of kids who are fully committed to God one day and doubt His existence the next. At camp they decide to become missionaries in Africa and later in the week they are caught smoking in the wilderness or making out with the girl (or guy) they just met.

The experimental phase of adolescence doesn't just affect moral behaviors like drinking and sexual promiscuity. It is also a major factor in developing a solid faith. As teens figure out and begin to own their faith, it can get pretty rough for parents who desire to pass on their own faith. A teenager's faith is often contradictory and self-centered. What teenager hasn't prayed to God to give them a better grade on a test because they didn't have time to study? Or blamed

A teenager's faith is often contradictory and self-centered.

God for not helping them find a date for the prom? The teen years can be filled with "I don't want to go to church anymore because it's boring and irrelevant." For others, like Cathy and me when we were growing up, the teen years were the spiritual formation time where we were converted and called to a lifelong ministry. Even so, that didn't stop us from drawing outside the lines with our teen beliefs and behaviors.

Just like a roller coaster ride, parents of teens have to tighten their seat belts and hold on for dear life. At the same time, understand that you can establish a foundation of faith in your teen's life with the spiritual tone you set for your family.

YOU SET THE PACE

Mark Holmen, a family ministry expert, tells a story about his days as a youth worker. He gave the students in his church a questionnaire to fill out in order to establish how much his ministry had influenced their faith. He laughingly says he thought it might help the church leadership consider raising his salary. The results weren't what Mark expected. By far the most significant influence was moms, with dads in a distant second, followed by grandparents, other relatives, siblings, and friends. Similar findings have been found in more formal studies. This is not to downplay the incredibly important place youth ministry can have in the lives of students, but rather to remind us that as parents we set the spiritual pace for our kids, for good or for bad.[1]

In his excellent book on teen spirituality, *Soul Searching*, Christian Smith states, "Most teenagers and their parents may not realize it, but a lot of research in the sociology of religion suggests that the most important social influence in shaping young people's religious lives is the religious life modeled and taught by their parents."[2] When you think about it, it makes sense. Teens with parents who attend church regularly will also be inclined to attend church regularly. With a healthy faith modeled from home, kids will naturally develop more of a faith mindset.

The good news is that we do not need to be perfect parents

and raise perfect kids. That would be discouraging. Teens today are looking for authenticity more than anything else, and it is possible to model a life of integrity even in the midst of developing your own spiritual life. When the Bible says "The man [or woman] of integrity walks securely" (Proverbs 10:9), the assumption is that if you live your life with integrity, not only will you have a more secure life, but so will your children. According to research authority George Barna, parents are beginning to understand that they have the primary responsibility for teaching their children spiritual values. He shared in a recent HomeWord radio interview that 85 percent of parents believe they have the primary task of teaching their children about spiritual beliefs and spiritual matters. However, he also found that the majority of parents do not spend any time during a typical week discussing spiritual matters or studying religious materials with their children. This disconnect is alarming and yet understandable. It's difficult to take the time to lead our children in spiritual principles when we are either too busy or too distracted.

Wayne Rice, in his most excellent book on spiritual legacy, *Generation to Generation*, says, "Busyness also keeps a lot of parents from being the spiritual leaders of their families. That's why the job so often gets outsourced to the church."[3] It is alarming how many well-intentioned parents will pour decades of intense effort into developing their children's ability to play soccer, gymnastics, or a band instrument and yet completely ignore the spiritual dimension. Obviously it's complicated, and there are other reasons besides being too busy, but the point remains: The primary task of spiritual training comes from home, with the church having a very important role of coming alongside the family, not in place of the family.

The biblical method of transmitting faith to the next

generation is quite clear. The Hebrews called it the *Shema*. Found in Deuteronomy 6:4–9, the Shema is still the most often quoted Scripture. Recited every morning and evening in Orthodox Jewish homes, it is also the standard for our Christian faith:

> Hear, O Israel: The Lord our God, the Lord is one. Love the Lord your God with all your heart and with all your soul and with all your strength. These commandments that I give you today are to be upon your hearts. Impress them on your children. Talk about them when you sit at home and when you walk along the road, when you lie down and when you get up. Tie them as symbols on your hands and bind them on your foreheads. Write them on the doorframes of your houses and on your gates.

Notice that the Shema teaches three key elements of faith: loyalty to God, transmission of your faith to your children, and even how you should daily go about sharing your faith with your family. The key to transmitting your faith is found in verse 6: "These commandments that I give you today are to be upon your hearts." Then, only after you nurture your own loyalty to God can you "impress them on your children."

Excitement for God and His Word is caught, not just taught. Children see, children do. If our children watch us cut corners and compromise integrity over and over again, why wouldn't they do the same? If our children see us carrying out an authentic faith development, they will most likely want to follow in our footsteps. When my daughter Christy was eight, she was sitting in our living room reading a little devotional book. When I asked her what she was doing, she answered, "I'm pretending I'm Mommy." Why? She had seen Cathy sit in the same place reading her devotional day after day.

HELPING MAKE FAITH AN ADVENTURE

The most effective way to help your children grow in their faith is by joining them in the journey and making faith an adventure. I love how C. S. Lewis expressed it in *The Lion, the Witch and the Wardrobe*. Young Lucy asks the Beavers if the godlike figure Aslan is safe. "Safe?" said Mr. Beaver. . . . "Who said anything about safe? Course he isn't safe. But he's good. He's the King, I tell you." Too many teenagers view their faith as dry, boring, and not relevant to their own personal lives. We have to help them see that this life adventure of faith is not necessarily the easy road, but it's the right one. Help your children understand that faith is a fun adventure. We can build beautiful memories and experiences that fit with what Jim Rayburn, the founder of Young Life, was fond of saying: "It's a sin to bore a kid with the gospel."

When my two oldest daughters became teenagers, I took them to Mexico to do mission work. We worked hard building a church. The dirt and sweat and calluses on our hands were not what I or they were used to. I kept wondering if they were having an okay time. One night we snuck away from the group and got some tacos from a street vendor. I had studied at the University of Mexico one summer, so I knew enough Spanish to be dangerous in ordering the food. What I remember most from the trip was how hot it was— and that each of us got sick from those street tacos. (In fact, my wife reminded me the other day of what a poor decision it was to venture out on our own!) What's amazing, though, is just this week Cathy and I flew back from the beautiful country of Ecuador, where one of those daughters now lives as part of an eight-month mission experience. During our visit, we talked more with our daughter about why she had decided to serve in a developing country. The first thing she mentioned was our time together serving in Mexico.

Every family can find ways to serve the poor and oppressed. I am always amazed how teenagers come through when they are physically and spiritually challenged to move beyond their comfort zone and make a difference in the lives of others. Even the most self-centered teenager is inclined to move beyond himself or herself and perhaps have their heart break with what breaks the heart of God.

SPIRITUAL DISCIPLINE

I've always been intrigued by the advice Paul gave to his protégé Timothy: "Discipline yourself for the purpose of godliness" (1 Timothy 4:7 NASB). Another version of that same advice from the Bible is, "Train yourself to be godly" (NIV). Teaching our children spiritual disciplines, and in a sense training them to honor God, is something that can be done. It was Henri Nouwen who once said, "A spiritual life without discipline is impossible. Discipline is the other side of discipleship."[4] Somehow the fine line between training and discipline is teaching our children to love God out of a response for what He has done for them and not just because they feel some sense of family responsibility.

I did an experiment several years ago with a Christian high school. It cost me about $750, but it was well worth the expense. I was speaking to the students on the power of prayer and devotions. I don't remember the talk being particularly exciting or motivating to these students, but at the end of the message I decided to present a fifty-day challenge. I asked them to commit to spending five to ten minutes of devotional time with God for fifty days straight. If they took my challenge, I would buy lunch for everyone who accomplished it. Even while explaining the details, my mind moved to the fact that since I wasn't very disciplined as a high school student, especially with devotions, they wouldn't be either. I figured I would have no problem buying lunch for the few students who might meet my challenge. Even when more than one hundred students took the challenge, I still didn't think it would cost me much. After all, I knew that youthful commitment often doesn't follow through. Well, fifty days later I got a list of eighty-three students who succeeded with my challenge. My first thought was of joy that they had attained an amazing goal. The second was, *My wife is going to kill me!* Even a cheap lunch was going to cost a lot! I ended up taking five to six kids at a time to lunch at a nearby Mexican restaurant. I really enjoyed hearing what they learned during the challenge, and it was great to recommend more tools to help them with their devotional life. In just fifty days they had established a wonderful habit. And no, Cathy didn't "kill me." She and I both agreed it was one of the best investments we could make in the lives of young people.

We mostly focus on breaking our kids' bad habits, but what would happen if we encouraged good and life-changing habits?

Studies show that if we spend twenty-five days doing most anything, it can become a habit. Another twenty-five days will solidify that activity for life. We mostly focus on breaking our kids' bad habits, but what would happen if we encouraged good and life-changing habits?

FAMILY FAITH CONVERSATIONS

One of the difficult findings about teens and faith in recent years is that a majority of teens who graduate from high school do not attend church the following year. There are several reasons for this, and youth ministry experts are searching for answers to change this downhill trend. However, Richard Ross of Southwestern Baptist Seminary has come up with a very positive insight from a study he did on teens and spirituality. Ross says teens are three times more apt to stay in church after they graduate from high school if there are healthy faith conversations within the home on a regular basis. Faith conversations are discussions and study about God and the Christian life in what feels like a spontaneous conversation. Parents can use media, the news, and discussion around the dinner table to bring up issues that pertain to faith. Faith conversations can also take place in a more formal "family time" setting on a weekly or regular basis.

A commitment to regular family devotions is not going to come from the kids, but if parents will take it seriously and develop family times together, it really can make a difference. We found with our own kids that they did better when it was a short, non-lecture format. We have found that the families that seem to do best keep these times fairly light and bring in another aspect of family fun time, whether it's fun food or a Wii bowling contest after the devotional time. The best faith conversations come when the kids see their parents as fellow learners, as opposed to the teacher-to-student role.

And don't feel pressure to come up with ideas for your family's faith conversations. There are plenty of good resources out there to use and adapt. If you feel a bit lost, just ask your local youth worker or children's worker for ideas.[5] The practical side of developing faith conversations at home is you can integrate a greater desire to study God's Word together, search practical topics from a biblical worldview, and spend time in prayer together.

After several decades of excellent research and study, we can now see that there are very positive outcomes with young people who have a positive spiritual experience in their teen years. From an academic study, Christian Smith found benefits in the areas of morals and values, healthy role models, spiritual empowerment, community and leadership, coping skills, choosing healthy relationships, and social and organizational skills.[6] This, of course, comes from academic research, but the true test is that when young people have a healthy spiritual life, they make better decisions about their friendships, school, sexuality, and obedience to authority, and they tend to experience much fewer at-risk behaviors. For this reason alone, do what you can to engage your kids on a spiritual level and stay engaged through even the later teenage years.

FAITH DEVELOPMENT AND TEENS

As children move from a more concrete way of thinking toward abstract, it is not uncommon for them to struggle with their faith. That is what happened with TJ. One day he told his parents he didn't want to go to church anymore. He said he didn't believe in God like he used to, plus he thought church was boring and irrelevant. His mom and dad were crushed and didn't know what to do: Should they force him to go to church? Try to debate him with his newfound atheism?

I asked if I could meet with TJ. It was clear that he was a bit unmotivated about life, but he respected his parents and wasn't antagonistic. All in all, he seemed like a good kid. I looked for deeper issues such as a major sin, broken relationship with parents, abuse, or anything that might cause his negative feelings about his faith. It just wasn't there. The main thing he expressed was not understanding how a loving God would allow things like death and war and poverty and abuse in the world. My response seemed to surprise him.

"I think your questioning is healthy."

"Really?"

"Yes. You're asking great questions for someone your age," I told him. "I've had many of those same questions, and sometimes they creep back into my mind."

"My parents think there's something wrong with me."

I replied, "The only thing wrong would be if you quit searching for the right answers to these really important questions." I then added, "I do wonder if your perception of the irrelevancy of church is more about your attitude rather than the church, because I know a number of people who really like your church." He smiled but said nothing.

I then offered TJ my fifty-day challenge. "How about investing five minutes a day for the next fifty days to your spiritual quest, and then meet with me every two weeks to talk?" I handed him my devotional book *Addicted to God*, and he took my challenge. By the time we met next, he had gone back to church and even had some dialog with his parents about faith. Today, TJ is a young adult with a very strong faith.

Just because teenagers seem bored with their faith, it doesn't mean they hate God.

As parents we have to remember that just because teenagers seem bored with their faith, it doesn't mean they hate God. TJ was actually going through a healthy way of disowning his parents' faith in order to develop a stronger faith of his own. The questions and convictions were all part of growing up spiritually. In fact, it would probably be wise for churches to teach more about faith development and spiritual formation. Let me explain.

James Fowler, a pioneer in the field of faith development, identified six stages of faith.[7] At stage one, children simply take on the faith of their parents. It's a simple faith, and mainly they mimic their parents' attitudes and even their prayers. At stage two, children start to connect faith to their church community and extended family, but it is still close to their parents' belief system. At stage three, their faith is not personalized as much as we think, but they are taking on the faith of their church or denomination. Stage four is what Fowler called the "individual stage." This means their faith is now their own. Sometimes they even move a bit outside the faith style of those closest to them. At this stage, faith is usually a bit simplistic and yet a serious commitment. Stage five is when children embrace some of the paradoxes of their faith. They are not shattered by unanswered prayer or the apparent suffering in the world that seems to be ever present. Their faith level is actually healthy, but a bit more complicated. The last stage, stage six, involves a more complex state of faith that often doesn't solidify until adulthood. Children develop their mission in life and sense of calling.

My hope is that by being aware of the normal stages of faith in a child's spiritual formation, you can relax a bit when your teen expresses doubts and questions. This isn't the time to preach, but rather it is an opportunity to explore together the issues in question.

SPIRITUAL LEGACY

At HomeWord, we often talk about how one of the purposes of the church is to mentor parents. Parents then mentor their children, and the legacy of faith continues from generation to generation. Producing a generational faith is never easy. Your teens may be far along the faith development road or just beginning. You can have two children, and at a certain age they will approach their faith from a totally different point of view. Along the way it takes a commitment to the daily task of faithfully following through on your commitments and pursuing with integrity your own spiritual life.

On our refrigerator at home, along with all the family photos, magnets, and the rest, we have a quote from Abraham Lincoln. I read it often as I think about my life, my marriage, and the spiritual legacy I want to leave my children. Although President Lincoln said these words almost a hundred and fifty years ago, they are still true today.

> Commitment is what transforms a promise into a reality. It is the words that speak boldly of your intentions, and the actions which speak louder than your words. It is making the time when there is none. Coming through time after time after time, year after year. Commitment is the stuff character is made of, the power to change the face of things. It is the daily triumph of integrity over skepticism.
>
> *Abraham Lincoln*

EIGHT

Dealing With a Troubled Teen

I hate you. I hate Jesus. Leave me alone.

Tracy, age 16

Never give up on someone. Miracles happen every day.

Author Unknown

One of the most difficult things in life is to see your child making poor choices. It can drag the whole family into emotional, spiritual, and even physical chaos. Every day at Home-Word we hear from desperate families who are looking for answers to their troubled teens. The parents are literally sick with worry, frustration, and anger. As I have said before, it's actually somewhat normal for teens to become secretive and argumentative and experimental in their behaviors. The challenge is figuring out what is normal adolescent rebellion and what goes deeper, where help is needed.

Some kids wander through adolescence almost untouched by the problems of the world, while others take the rocky road with steep hills to climb and dangerous curves at every turn. I see good parents who have troubled teens and really bad parents whose kids are amazingly healthy and stable.

If your family has been in crisis or you are dealing with a troubled teen, you know the depth of pain and the burden you carry. Some of the worst heartache and anguish in my life has come with the sorrow of my children's poor choices. At times I have blamed myself, my wife, the culture, and even our church. I have sat with hundreds of brokenhearted parents, so worn down by their teens that they don't know how they can make it through the week. When a child makes poor choices, it rips your heart out of your body.

Few parents see it coming. A troubled teen usually just sort of evolves with a bad decision here and a poor choice there. Then a misstep takes him or her in a really horrible direction. The next thing you know, your reality is different than you ever imagined possible.

Cathy and I have a friend who is a noted author and speaker in the area of youth and family. We know him well. He and his wife are people of integrity, role models for Christian leadership outside and inside their home. Yet their children have struggled with drug abuse, sexual promiscuity, lack of spiritual life, eating disorders, and even arrests. My friend once admitted to me that he was "stunned by the way things have turned out with the kids." It has affected his marriage, his vocation, and his health. Sure, a few bumps along the road were to be expected, but because he and his wife were in youth and family ministry, they fully believed their kids would turn out similar to the strongest leaders in his youth group. Not so. Whenever I see this couple, we sit and catch up. They really are suffering, and there is a general sadness in their countenance. Frankly, they have tried everything

I will suggest to you in this chapter. Their kids have been on antidepressants and gone through drug rehab, in-depth counseling, and intense Christian recovery programs. Life is not unbearable for these parents; they hold out hope—their story is not finished yet. But life sure hasn't turned out the way they thought or hoped it would.

There aren't any simple answers for dealing with troubled teens. However, through the years I have seen enough good stories and victories to not be discouraged.

If you have a troubled teen, let me shout from the rooftop: THERE IS HOPE! I see parents every day who work a plan and their teens turn around and use that adolescent bump (or bumps) in the road to become stronger and more successful with life than their parents ever will.

If you have a troubled teen, let me shout from the rooftop: THERE IS HOPE!

The story of Jack is a story of hope. Jack was never an easy child. At his first grade parent/teacher conference, his teacher reported that Jack was extremely smart but had difficulty focusing on his work and didn't always get along with classmates. Even so, he was very likable, she said, and would probably do just fine. Well, he didn't. The hyperactivity and lack of focus caused more and more problems, and a pediatrician finally diagnosed Jack with ADHD. His parents tried to keep him off medication, but eventually he was put on Ritalin. As Jack got older, things continued to spiral. Fights with other boys and lack of respect toward his parents seemed to be a way of life. One day Jack and his father squared off and Jack took a swing at his dad, yelling, "I hate this f——ing family, and I especially hate you." The out-of-control behavior resulted in Jack being sent to a boarding school in another state. There, he started to use marijuana, which led to other types of drug use. At the end of the school year, Jack moved back home and barely made it through the rest of high school. He tried community college, but dropped out the first semester and moved in with a girlfriend. His parents told me that as much as they were upset about Jack's poor choices, their home finally felt physically and emotionally safe. Over the years, they had tried counseling, the five months of boarding school, tough love, easing his restrictions, prayer groups, anything that might help.

One day, Jack's girlfriend told him she had been going to a Bible study at work and had renewed her commitment to God. With God's help, she was going to try to get off drugs and alcohol. And she wanted Jack to also deal with his addictions to drugs, alcohol, and pornography. She then told him she was going to live with her aunt who would encourage her renewed faith. Jack was stunned. He felt rejected, and over the next few weeks he went on a binge-drinking spree. His life got so bad that, just like the prodigal son in the Bible, Jack showed up at his parents' home one day. They lovingly allowed him to stay, but only under the condition that he would get help. They set up healthy boundaries and a very short list of expectations with grace and consequences.

Without going into the details, I can tell you that Jack was able to pull his life together, and today he is happily married and has two children. He is a pastor in a well-respected church and works with rebellious kids and hurting families. He is first to tell you that he is still dealing with baggage from those rebellious years, and that he has to work a plan for the rest of his life for sobriety and emotional and spiritual health.

As you might expect, though, his parents see Jack's amazing recovery as nothing short of answered prayer. He and his wife live near his parents, and they all enjoy a special, close relationship. Jack says, "If I can find healing, anyone can."

There are countless stories of out-of-control teens who are now living healthy, productive lives. They didn't immediately respond to help when they were younger. Perhaps they hated their parents, but they probably hated themselves too. They knew their behavior was out of control, but they weren't ready to change. Usually the answer lies in the fact that a courageous parent or parents did the right work to help the child get to a place of healing.

WHAT CAN A PARENT DO?

Many parents get to a place of conflict with their children. So if your home feels like an emotional war zone, you are not alone and you are not imagining things. The tension affects every aspect of the family and strains every relationship.

When your child is going through a difficult season, I advise the same starting point as mentioned in chapter 1: *Stay as calm as you possibly can, get on the same page with your spouse, and get as emotionally, spiritually, and physically healthy as you possibly can.*

Persevere and Seek God's Help

It is interesting that Jesus spoke more about trouble and suffering than he did about human happiness. The challenges and crisis of a prodigal child can tax us to the very end of our strength. The answer lies in living one day at a time and persevering through life's darkest hours with power rooted in God's compassion and mercy. The Bible is clear that even in life's most painful and difficult times, we can keep going because God is with us. His mercy endures forever. I especially like Psalm 136, which reminds us that through tough times we can "give thanks to the Lord, for he is good. *His love endures forever*" (verse 1, emphasis added). Ruth Graham, the amazing woman of God and wife to evangelist Billy Graham, wrote a prayer once in the midst of tough times with her own children. She called it "A Mother Is Praying."[1]

> Listen, Lord,
> a mother's praying
> low and quiet:
> listen, please.
> Listen what her tears
> are saying,
> see her heart
> upon its knees;
> lift the load
> from her bowed shoulders
> till she sees
> and understands,
> You, who hold
> the worlds together,
> hold her problems
> in Your hands.

God would never want you to go through the burden of a troubled teen alone. Throughout the Bible, He promises to be there for His children. He doesn't promise to take away all of our trials and tribulations, but He does promise to walk with us through the darkest of valleys. Many people find comfort in reading through the inspiring songbook of the Hebrew people, Psalms, or the promises of the book of Proverbs. Others find hope and comfort in listening to worship music and filling their hearts with praise. This is not the time to turn away from God in disappointment, but as Ruth Graham's prayer says, it is time to put your trust in Him and place your children into His care. Since He was there at the miracle of conception, He cares deeply about your prodigal child.

Find Support

When trouble hits the home, too many people try to hide it. Some look at their child's behavior as shameful to the whole family. The way I figure it, every family struggles and suffers with a family issue at one time or another. We were not meant to carry our burdens alone. Our pride often gets in the way and we don't want to share our pain even with a trusted friend. That is just wrong.

I love the story of the Israelites battling the Amalekites in the Old Testament. Moses stands on a hill during the battle and raises his hands toward heaven. As long as he holds up his hands, the Israelites are winning the battle. But Moses gets weary and lowers his hands. Immediately the Amalekites begin to defeat the people of Israel. So Moses makes a really good decision. In his weariness, he allows the people around him to help hold up his hands, and the Israelites eventually win the battle. The same illustration goes for parents of a troubled teen. You need to find people who won't necessarily take your burden away. Usually they can't do that. But they can help you carry this burden. Maybe it's a regular coffee appointment with a mentor from your church or a couples/parent gathering. All around the country there are support groups for parents of troubled teens. It may not be easy, but seek support. Don't be afraid to tell a trusted friend your burden.

Get on the Same Page With Your Spouse

When there is a rebellious teen in the house, it's natural to play the blame game. And the easiest person to blame is your spouse. This is true if you are a single parent focusing on the faults of your ex, or if you are married. However, this is not the time to make the problems of your spouse the focal point. It is so easy to do, but it will only distract you from the more important issues. If a couple has a game plan they can agree upon, they will do much better. Many parents have never read a parenting book or attended a parenting class together. More women read books like this one than men. But when there is a crisis, I urge couples to develop a parenting philosophy together. This is especially a time when they need to work off the same blueprint. "United we stand, divided we fall" applies to parenting too. If you are working off the same page, it will bring security to your child, and definitely two heads, hearts, and mouths are better than one in this situation. If you can't get on the same page, then make sure you personally have a philosophy of parenting that you are following.[2]

I speak to thousands of people a year in parenting seminars, and one of the practical questions always asked is, "Which parenting philosophy do you recommend?" I'm not sure people like my answer. I tell them to find one that works for them. Good parenting philosophies are a bit like good diets. Basically the way to lose weight is through the discipline of exercise and healthy diet. Sure, there are all kinds of fads and different approaches, but any good weight-loss program includes a healthy dose of exercise and right kind of eating. Well, the same is true for good parenting. Parenting books often focus on a particular parenting style, but the good parenting philosophies all generally have the same key themes. So find a philosophy that works for you. The interesting part about human nature is that what might work for one child has to be tweaked for the next one.[3]

Develop a Contract for Behavior

I have seen many parents, worn down from out-of-control behavior, seek a quick fix. They immediately look into sending their teen to a rehab or boarding school. Seldom is this the answer. Helping a troubled teen is a process, and sending them away is not always the best solution. I strongly believe that the first step is to develop a contract together. Sometimes a change in behavior comes with something as simple as putting a road map in front of your child that clearly defines rules, consequences, and goals. The contract becomes a wake-up call and stops certain behaviors before they get more out of control. I always suggest that you try to create the contract with your child and identify good and bad consequences together. Put the contract in writing and see what happens. As mentioned earlier, kids will more likely support what they help to create. Creating a contract together gives you the opportunity to show more empathy. Still, make sure you follow through on the contract. Gradually (but not too gradually) make the consequences tougher and tougher. If they continue to break the contract, I recommend getting an assessment.

Get an Assessment

An assessment is simply a thorough checkup on whatever situation or problems are going on with your teen and family. It really isn't much different than going to your medical doctor to get a comprehensive examination for a health problem. An assessment isn't a long-term counseling commitment, but rather it's trying to get to the root of the issue to develop a go-forward plan. Depending on what the issue is with your teen, an assessment could be as simple as visiting your school counselor for an academic evaluation. A tougher issue might require a much more involved psychological, medical, and even spiritual assessment. What is complicated and challenging to you may not be to a person who does regular assessments. For example, I used to do drug and alcohol assessments of young people, and I would ask several key questions and usually have an answer for the young person and parents in one session.[4]

It's pretty amazing to see the kids who are literally transformed to a much better place because of an assessment with an easily diagnosed problem. "Lights have turned on" in their brain when they and their parents find out about a learning disability or a physical issue that can be easily addressed. Even with a more complicated diagnosis, just knowing what the issue is and having a plan in place can do wonders for a troubled teen and their family.

Some assessments don't bring good news. After a very honest conversation with a sixteen-year-old about his regular habit of smoking pot and drinking, I asked if he wanted to change his behavior. "Not really," he responded. I told him I appreciated his honesty, and I invited him to call me on my cell phone when he was ready or had hit bottom. Later, when I met with his dad, I said, "I'm so sorry, but your son is just not ready today to get the help he needs or to make the right decisions about his drug and alcohol use and abuse." We then talked about how to apply tough love to the situation and help "create a crisis" to help the son reach out to get the help he needed.

Seek Counsel From an Expert

Many times after an assessment, counseling is a good option. The Bible says, "Where there is no counsel a people fall, but in the multitude of counselors there is safety" (Proverbs 11:14).

One of the strongest and healthiest Christ-followers I know is a good friend of mine, Henry Cloud. Henry is one of the most influential psychologists in the world today. One day when we were having breakfast together and just talking about life, I asked, "Henry, how did you get to have such a profound spiritual faith?" His answer reminded me why counseling can be so good. He smiled and said, "I have learned more about God through the trials and tribulations of my clients. I view my role not so much as a counselor but rather as a discipler of people."

Some kids who are troubled need a neutral, safe person to talk with, someone who understands what they are going through and can help them get to a better place. Find a counselor who is good with students; some counselors work better with adults. Make sure your teen can identify with his or her counselor. For many troubled teens, a professional counselor is best. However, pastors, youth workers, teachers, and even coaches can counsel and influence your son or daughter.

With a teen who is struggling, counseling often becomes a family affair, and there are times when the whole family should be involved. Also, parents can be helped greatly when they seek counsel for just themselves. Cathy and I have often used the wisdom of a counselor to gain perspective on a kid-related issue. Seeking counseling is a sign of strength, not a sign of weakness.

Seeking counseling is a sign of strength, not a sign of weakness.

Here are five tips for finding the right counselor for your situation.

1. *Ask a trusted friend or pastor for a recommendation.* People who have had positive experiences with counseling can be a good resource for finding the right counselor.

2. *Whenever possible have a brief phone conversation with potential counselors before you make an appointment.* Speaking with a counselor before you make an appointment provides a good opportunity to sense whether you or your child will be able to create a sense of rapport with the prospective counselor.

3. *Ask the right questions in your brief phone call.* Ask about experience with your issue. Ask about costs upfront. In a sense, look at the phone call as if you are interviewing the counselor, more than getting help for your problem. Briefly state your issue, but focus on getting to know the counselor.

4. *Choose a counselor and take him or her for a "test drive."* You can often tell if you connect with a counselor in the first or second session.

5. *Evaluate the first session.* Make your longer-term decisions after you have met with the counselor. There is a difference between a few sessions of receiving wisdom and counsel and long-term therapy. Can you see yourself or your teen spending several sessions with this counselor?

RESIDENTIAL FACILITIES

Excellent residential facilities are available for struggling teenagers, but they are not a quick fix. In fact, in most cases, a facility should be a last resort after other options have failed.

If your teenager is totally out of control and experiencing ongoing self-destructive behavior, it is time to consider a change of environment and an extreme intervention. Most teen boarding and rehabilitation facilities are expensive, but they really do a good job. It's difficult to make good decisions in the face of a crisis, so I suggest doing homework on residential programs when your teen is beginning some out-of-control behavior. Here are some questions to ask:

- Does the program specialize in your child's key problem? For example, if your child has an eating disorder, look for effective facilities that specialize in eating disorders.
- Do you want a rehabilitation center that is based on the Christian faith?
- What does the educational component look like?
- Is there a customized family training module?
- How much does it cost?
- Are any parts of treatment covered by insurance?

Make your list of facility options. Do your homework. Ask lots of questions. Speak to parents who have sent their kids to the facility you are looking at, and also look at who endorses the program.

The fearless Masai warriors of Africa greet each other with an interesting question: "How are the children?" The traditional response carries a lot of meaning: "All the children are well." Their commitment to caring for the young members of their society is strong.

Today, in our country, could it be said that the children are not well? Frankly, until all kids are free of abuse and addictions, we must do everything in our power to come alongside them. It has never been easier for teenagers to slip through the cracks of society. With various addictions so prevalent, very good families have kids who are hurting and making really bad choices. Hurting parents feel the pain, guilt, and despair of their child not being well.

The good news is, no matter what the issue, hope and transformation can be around the corner. Don't suffer in silence, but rather seek whatever help you need for this journey. And remember: *Never* give up on someone. Miracles happen every day.

NINE

Your Marriage and Raising Teens

I ran too fast, too far, too long on too many borrowed
miles. And then it hit me like something just plain awful.
I have been a psychological, spiritual, and emotional mess.
I need to refine my life, my marriage, and my parenting
so I can live again.

A mother of three teenagers

A successful marriage is an edifice that must be rebuilt
every day.

André Maurois

"I'm just not connecting with you right now." These seem
to be common words of people who are married and raising
teenagers. The couples are usually very good people, trying their best to survive and wishing for a kinder, gentler
season in life. They love each other, but if they are really
honest, they aren't sure if they are "in love." Or, at least,
it doesn't feel like it used to. They are tired most of the

time. Their conversations seem to center around the kids, and now that the kids are teens, they have more worries. One mom confided to me, "I just have a genuine sadness deep inside me. I didn't think it would turn out this way. My husband is a good man, but he isn't my soul mate. I would never leave him, but I guess I've just settled for a lifestyle with little connection, and deep inside of me I have sorrow."

Jenny and Brad are also missing that connection in their marriage. On the outside, they are an amazing couple. They have three beautiful teenagers, and from the looks of their Christmas card and letter, they are the perfect family. Todd is nineteen, Andrew is sixteen, and Ashley is thirteen. Todd was the star athlete in high school and graduated with honors. Andrew is following in his brother's footsteps and his father's before that. Ashley is the princess of the family and has her mother's good looks and her father's charm. Jenny helps lead the school's PTA, teaches a Bible study at her church, and hasn't missed one of her kids' games or gymnastic tournaments. She has a part-time home decorating business and people marvel at how she juggles it all. Brad runs a successful business, but managed to coach the boys in all their sports. At times he has to miss a few gymnastic events, but even then, he makes sure to call Ashley before and after the meets. These are good people with amazing intentions. Except one thing. Behind the Christmas letter and perfect family photo, trouble is brewing.

Jenny and Brad are living parallel lives. They are exhausted all the time. No one is managing the bills very well, and even though they make a lot of money, their debt is piling up. They can't remember when just the two of them went away for a replenishing time of romance. Life centers on the kids, work, and everyday commitments and responsibilities. They crawl into bed each night, six inches away from each other but miles apart relationally. The word that describes how they feel toward each other is *numb*. As for the kids, each has at least one major issue. Todd is a nice young man, but two months into college, he got a DUI that will be on his record for the next ten years. Andrew has been caught smoking pot and visits porn sites regularly. Beautiful Ashley has the beginning signs of an eating disorder. The Christmas photo and letter was only half this family's story.

Jenny and Brad have five to seven more years of a teenager living in the home. They might be looking ahead, counting on reconnecting after the storms of adolescence clear out. But while their marriage is suffering, they are also missing out on opportunities to model a healthy relationship to their kids.

Most marriages don't end because of abuse, adultery, or addictions; more commonly, they just fade away. The couple quits paying attention to the basics of a healthy marriage, they drift from each other because of the many distractions around them, and one day they look up and see a marriage that is lost.

This book is not meant to be a marriage book. And, frankly, many single parents do a wonderful job raising their teenagers. But most single parents would agree that it would be easier to handle the teen years with a spouse. This season with teens seems to bring an extra amount of tension and stress into a marriage. Instead of a couple leaning into each other, they tend to grow apart. It does not have to be so.

Let's look at the stressors of a marriage during the teen years and how to overcome them.

SMOLDERING STRESS

Has stress and busyness pushed you into a danger zone with your life and marriage? Many families with teenagers are living life at 120 percent. Physician and author Richard Swenson described this situation to me during a HomeWord radio program. "Today, most of us routinely spend 20 percent more than we have, whether in money, time, or energy," he said. "When life is continually maximized, however, there is no margin for priorities, relationship, depth, worship, rest, contemplation, service, or healing."

Everything is more dangerous at high speed, and eventually, if we continue life at high speed, something is going to spin out of control and crash. Often it is the marriage, the kids, and our relationship with God. Normally these should be our three top priorities, but crisis-mode living and stress tend to smother what's most important. It would be better for families to live at 80 percent and have margin for the unexpected. Living with margin takes some of the most focused discipline you can imagine, especially when there is so much being thrown at us from every direction, but it is possible to make the necessary changes.

Crisis-mode living and stress tend to smother what's most important.

In Jillian's case, her husband wasn't taking the lead, so she did. Without lecturing or nagging, Jillian made three decisions that brought back a sense of rhythm to the family and her marriage. Jillian established a nonnegotiable date night with her husband every week. She would have loved for him to come up with the idea, but he just wasn't the type of guy to be proactive in this area of their relationship.

Then, she let the kids choose just one extracurricular activity each season instead of all the activities and "stuff" that had the family running around so much. And finally, she made Sundays a very different-looking day of the week for the family, a much more restful day.

Jillian's husband wasn't opposed to the date night idea at all. She made sure the kids were taken care of those nights and planned fun and enjoyable dates that quickly became the highlight of the week and rekindled their romance. The kids first balked at participating in fewer activities, but Jillian stood her ground. There were more family dinners and less stress almost immediately. The most difficult change for the family was the Sunday activity load. When Jillian was growing up, her family held to a Sabbath, which means rest. Even as a child she looked forward to a special family meal after church on Sunday, and then much of the rest of the day was geared toward slowing down the pace of life. For her family, Jillian instituted a "technology disconnect" as part of their Sunday routine. Cell phones would stay in their chargers except for an emergency, and the computer was off-limits except for schoolwork. As much as possible, they made Sundays family fun days. There were still ups and downs for the family each week—stress didn't disappear—but Jillian's initiatives helped to nourish their relationships, and margin slowly moved back into the family.

Busyness can seem necessary and unavoidable in today's world, but it so easily becomes a habit that takes over a family's life. You look up one day and realize that you have quietly and unintentionally been disconnecting from those you love the most, including God, and replaced what is precious with whatever is most pressing. When we are tired and exhausted, discouragement creeps in more easily. Are you taking care of your own soul? What are you doing to enhance your marriage? Do you have replenishing relationships around you to support you and keep you accountable when needed?

There was a time in the prophet Elijah's life when he was so tired and discouraged that he wanted to just give up (see 1 Kings 19). What did he do? He went to sleep. After he slept, God sent an angel to give him something to eat and drink, and then he went back to sleep again. Only after he was rested and refreshed was he ready to take on the day. Maybe, like Elijah, we need to get more rest.

REKINDLING ROMANCE

Couples with teenagers around the house often roll their eyes when the subject of romance is brought up. They look back at another time in the relationship as a time with more physical intimacy. Too many couples have settled for mediocrity in their marriage, and frankly, are just lazy when it comes to romancing each other.

When I am driving, I periodically listen to a radio host who says it like it is when it comes to relationships. If a caller says the spark is gone in their marriage, the host usually interrupts and asks, "Are you treating your husband like a boyfriend?" Or, "Does your wife know she is your girlfriend?"

It seems like when we were dating and courting our spouse, we could find time and energy for them. We did special little things for them. Romantic love does change over the years, but it doesn't have to slow to a crawl. Someone in the relationship is going to have to decide to *initiate romance*. I know that sounds a bit unromantic and not spontaneous. If the romance in your marriage is good now, then by all means keep doing whatever you are doing. But if it is not working how you want, then be more intentional.

When the kids were younger, you could put them to bed early, perhaps light a fire in the fireplace, and snuggle with your spouse. With teens, you quite possibly may be going to bed earlier than they do now. We know a couple who took a massage class together at the local community college, and Friday nights are now massage nights for each other. A regular, nonnegotiable date night is a must. Cathy and I also choose to go away four times a year, sometimes even for just one night. Concerts, walks in the park, flowers, special meals, love notes, and phone calls are all a part of keeping the spark in your marriage. The good thing about having teenagers is that they can usually take care of themselves, so it is easier to find special times with your spouse.

MONEY: THE BIG STRESSOR

As my father used to always say, "The best things in life aren't things." In the midst of saving for college and weddings, as well as just trying to keep the budget working, money is one of the major stressors in a marriage with teens. The majority of people choose debt over financial freedom. What they may not be thinking about is that debt will cause pressure on a marriage like few other stressors.

When Barry and Sharon bought a great house with a larger monthly payment than they could really afford, they didn't realize the extra strain it would put on their marriage.

They were already juggling needy kids and a needy mother-in-law, yet what kept them awake nights was the house payment and all the related upkeep. When they finally went to a marriage counselor, he promptly suggested they see a financial consultant from their church. When he asked about their budget, they said they didn't have one in writing but "pretty much" knew how they spent their money. After putting together a budget, there was still no margin. Barry and Sharon basically had two choices. Both of them worked full time, so Barry could get a second job or they could move to a cheaper home. Before they made a decision, the wise financial counselor said, "Don't just look at making your payments, but look at the quality of life with your teenagers and with your marriage." In the end, they sold their home, moved into a smaller rental, set up a budget that allowed 10 percent for giving and 10 percent for saving, paid off most of their bills, and now say it's the best decision of their marriage. "I grieved about giving up my dream of that house, but our kids really don't care, and Barry and I have our marriage back on track," Sharon said. "We didn't realize how much negative energy we were putting into our financial struggles."

When faced with spending more than you make versus investing in your marriage and family, choose what's most important. The answer to the money pit issue is to be a faithful steward of your resources. Do what it takes to steer clear of financial burdens. If it means moving to a smaller house or purchasing a cheaper car or taking a camping vacation rather than an exotic one, by all means do what you can to stay free from the bondage of debt. Delayed gratification is the key to financial maturity.

"NOTHING LIKE TWO TEENS AND A CONFUSED MOTHER-IN-LAW"

Just today a good friend e-mailed me the sentiment above. He and his wonderful wife are in the midst of what some would call the terrible teen years. Their son is struggling with ADD and is medicating his problems with drugs and alcohol. Their daughter is constantly at odds with her mother. It is a tension-filled home for this season. On top of it, Grandma has Alzheimer's and had to move in with them. It made me weary just hearing their story.

Many married couples with teens are sandwiched between what can be two needy groups: their kids and their aging parents. For as long as there have been mothers-in-law, there have been the jokes, but frankly, many marriages are torn apart every year because of the in-law/outlaw situation.

When I do premarital counseling, I always spend one of the early sessions on the couple's extended family. We do a fun (or not so fun) exercise of filling out a family map. It brings to light their extended family, and we find out the "dirt" on some of the characters in the family. How will those characters interact with the couple's relationship? We talk about overcoming negative family patterns and divorce and addictions and whatever else comes up. At some point I typically ask, "Have you ever thought what you'd do if one of your parents needed to move in with you and you'd have to take care of them?" The looks and responses are almost funny. I've never had anyone say yes. But I know that by the time they are married and their children are teens, there is a good chance there will be some in-law issues to negotiate as a couple.

Some marriages are blessed with amazing in-laws and

some just are not. To tell a young couple that they are kind of, sort of marrying into the other family is almost not worth talking about, because many young couples don't understand the concept. Still, as people live longer, the sandwich generation of parents raising their teens while also helping out their own parents is getting bigger.

With this in-law issue in mind, it's important to talk about and establish expectations. Of course, you can't come up with all the answers ahead of time, but the more you talk through things and get on the same page, the better. Cathy's mom and dad lived five hours away when our children were teenagers. As her dad's Alzheimer's progressed, Cathy spent quite a lot of time helping them out. Cathy modeled for our daughters amazing commitment to her parents. We knew the frequent trips were for a season, and we knew it wouldn't be easy for any of us, so it was important to talk as a couple and share our needs and expectations. And we needed to do the same with our kids. As self-absorbed as teens can get, they will sometimes think about themselves more than you or their grandparent or other family members. What they need to see is a united front whenever possible, and they need to see you model love and commitment to your extended family.

LACK OF SPIRITUAL INTIMACY

It's a common surprise: Parents think that once their children get past the exhausting toddler years and become more independent, life will slow down and the couple will have more time to connect spiritually. For many, the opposite occurs. For whatever reason—busyness, tension in the relationship, stress, or another issue—couples can grow apart and miss out on spiritual intimacy.

Cathy and I met our first day of school at Azusa Pacific University. We were married one week after Cathy graduated. From the beginning, we knew we wanted to focus on doing youth and family ministry together. A year later we moved across the country so I could go to graduate school. With united hearts on ministry, we expected to have spiritual intimacy in our relationship. It didn't happen. We had good intentions—we tried everything from devotionals to prayer commitment times and couples Bible studies, and would usually start out strong—but then we would fail to have the discipline to continue. As the kids got older, our spiritual time together got less and less. In many ways, we were leading parallel lives spiritually, yet we both knew we were missing something as a couple.

One day we were talking with an older couple who had mentored us from time to time, and we told them of our frustrations. We expected they were the type of people who read through the Bible every year together and had long intimate prayer times daily. "Actually, you both might be setting yourself up for failure," they said. "We spend twenty to thirty minutes a week in a devotional time. Start with that and see how it goes." That conversation had a huge impact on us. And today, in addition to trying to pray together daily, we set aside a special time each week to get spiritually closer. We look at a Scripture together, read something short and inspirational, share our ideas about what we've read, and then pray. Our weekly times of spiritual connection even led us to write a devotional for other couples called *Closer*.

Dr. David Stoop, a leading authority on marriage, estimates that just one tenth of one percent of couples who pray together daily will get a divorce. I'm not trying to turn this into legalism, but having a devotional time once a week and praying together daily builds a foundation of spiritual intimacy that will draw a couple closer and prepare them for their life together, even after the kids leave home. Personally, I have found that because Cathy and I often come at parenting issues from a different angle, our devotional times and talks help to get us on the same page. So make it a goal to move toward true spiritual oneness. Jesus quoted the Old Testament when he said, "A man will leave his father and mother and be united to his wife and the two will become one flesh" (Matthew 19:5; Genesis 2:24). If this is your heart's desire, to become one flesh, do what it takes to connect physically, emotionally, *and* spiritually.

Unfortunately, the goal for many couples in this season of life is to simply get through the teen years. I don't think it has to be this way. Recently Cathy and I celebrated an anniversary by taking in a concert at the Hollywood Bowl in Southern California and spending the night nearby. That next day we reflected on our marriage and realized quite quickly that the success of our marriage was not the result of marrying the perfect person or always experiencing "the spark." Our success has come from working on our relationship, persevering, and striving to do what we thought was right. A successful marriage is not a gift, it is more like an achievement.

TEN

The Changing Culture

The math teacher asked Johnny, "What are 2, 4, 28, and 44?" Johnny quickly replied, "NBC, CBS, HBO, and the Cartoon Channel."

America today is a girl-destroying place. . . . Many girls lose contact with their true selves, and when they do, they become extraordinarily vulnerable to a culture that is all too happy to use them for its purposes.

Mary Pipher

Adults can protect boys from degrading, dehumanizing, and desensitizing images. This exposure is a corrupting influence on the foundations of moral development.

James Garbarino

Not long ago, a father in Denver hired a stripper to perform at his twelve-year-old son's birthday party. No doubt this shocks you as much as it does me. The problem is, lots of kids are experiencing this kind of thing over and over again—on the Internet. Of course, this father is a sick man and hopefully is getting the help and justice he needs. But today you cannot afford to sit back and allow the dark side of culture to become a major influence in your teen's life.

You may not look at your teen years as a cakewalk, but compared to what our kids are facing, it was a much kinder and gentler planet back then. I've mentioned that I grew up one block away from Disneyland. I walked to school and played in nearby orange groves long since replaced by strip malls and hotels. My friends and I were free to ride our bikes all around the neighborhood. All the neighbors knew each other and watched out for each other. Back then, teens certainly experimented with behaviors that weren't good or healthy for them, but not at such young ages as today's kids, and not with such dangerous risks. As I have said, "We were twelve, fourteen, and seventeen, but we were never *their* age."

I'm a very optimistic person, but the world our teens are growing up in is a mess. We can blame it on media, globalization, and a host of other issues, but our kids are no longer innocent. We can discuss it, complain, protest, and fight the establishment, but in the end, we are the ones who will have to make the adjustments and fight to keep a biblical worldview in front of our children.

Our culture is changing so quickly that even culture watchers have a difficult time keeping up. Of course, not all cultural changes are bad. Many are just different. For example, kids still crave relationships and community, but they will find those relationships and community in different ways than previous generations did. It's not their fault that society is rapidly changing.

Every year Beloit College publishes something they call

a "Mindset List."[1] The collection of cultural reference points shows how we have fewer shared experiences with each new crop of college freshmen. Some recent examples:

- "You sound like a broken record" has no meaning to them, because they never owned a record player.
- Tattoos and piercings have always been chic and highly visible.
- The Vietnam War is as ancient history as World War I, World War II, and the Civil War.
- There has always been MTV.
- They cannot fathom not having a remote control.
- Thongs no longer are worn on your feet.
- Bert and Ernie are old enough to be their parents.
- Photographs have always been processed in an hour or less and most are found on their computer.

The cartoon my wife handed me today shows a teenager lying on the floor in his bedroom. He is holding his iPhone, Skyping with his friend on the computer, and listening to music on his MP3 player. The TV is on in the background, and many other gadgets are around the room. As he talks with his friend via the computer, he apparently answers a question about how he is doing, saying, "Profoundly bored. What about you?" The response from his friend: "Same."

GETTING YOUR ARMS AROUND SHIFTING MINDSETS

A key theme of this book is how important it is to be a student of the culture. We do this not to become negative critics. Instead, it is to get our arms around who and what is influencing our kids. With this information, we can then teach them to discern right from wrong.

Entire books, magazines, and Web sites are devoted to culture watching. Any good book about raising teenagers today will have major sections dedicated to culture-related issues. In this chapter, I want to expand on earlier discussions regarding culture and media, but also talk about some of the newer challenges facing our kids today. There are principles that can help us help our kids navigate the culture in healthy ways.

HomeWord publishes a free weekly culture update for parents that is definitely worth reading on a regular basis. (To subscribe, visit www.homeword.com.) I read it every time I see it in my inbox. As a parent who wants to keep their arms around the culture, you will want to look at issues such as these:

- Kids and media use
- New studies show link between teen drug and alcohol use and increased sexual activity
- Teen Internet addicts more likely to self-harm
- How cyberbullying is affecting our children
- Texting and driving is more dangerous than drinking and driving
- New survey confirms one in five teens send (sext) sexual photos via texting
- Alcohol dependence linked to age of first drink
- Parents underestimate kid's social networking usage and behaviors

- Teens' heavy drinking is tied to depression
- Parents are key to preventing teen smoking
- Teenage jobless rate reaches record high
- SAT scores vary by race, gender, and family income
- Teens' credit card usage is way up
- Multigenerational family households make a comeback
- 90 percent of teens admit stronger likelihood of drinking and driving on prom night

These are but a few of the issues taken from headlines in the HomeWord Culture Brief. The point is clear: We must keep up with the latest cultural trends and how they are affecting our children. As I mentioned in the chapter on creating a media-safe home, we must read what they read, watch what they watch, and listen to what they listen to.

READ

One of the most effective ways to quickly learn about teenage culture is to read what they read. At times I have walked into our local public library, collected the various teen magazines, and sat down at a table and thumbed through them. The teen magazines are doing research on this generation and know exactly what is front and center in the minds of adolescents. So reading the articles can give you a handle on what your kids are talking about at school.

There are also lots of teen Web sites. Some of the information is pretty raw, but it may be worthwhile to look at a few sites to understand their influence. You should also know that trustworthy, safe information on youth culture is available on the Web. My personal favorite is Walt Mueller's Center for Parent/Youth Understanding (www.CPYU.org). Walt is one of the leading authorities on youth culture and does an excellent job helping parents navigate the culture from a Christian worldview. I also highly recommend Jim Liebelt's Youth Culture Watch (available at www.homeword.com).

WATCH

A major part of being a student of the culture is to watch what is influencing your teen. Cathy and I periodically rent popular teen movies to get a handle on what kids are watching. It also helps to occasionally watch TV shows and You-Tube videos that are popular at the time. Ask teens to see photos they have on their iPod or similar device. When you attend sporting, music, or other types of events at your child's school, notice how your teen interacts with his or her friends and pay close attention to how other teens their age act as well—what they talk about and wear and how they behave in general. In the days when I was directly involved in youth ministry, we called this "contact work," which is basically meeting young people in their territory, outside the walls of home and church. There are lots of opportunities to be in a teenager's territory. Be the parent who volunteers at youth activities or chaperons or drives. Some of my best learning experiences came when I quietly drove kids to events or served as a chaperon.

LISTEN

As I mentioned before, listening may be the best way to better understand your teen and his or her cultural influences. I learned quite quickly that my children didn't want me to act like a teenager and participate in their activities. However, it was okay to ask about what was happening in their world—as long as the questions weren't judgmental. Find times to ask your teen questions about school, music, drugs, alcohol use on campus, and any other issue. The more casual you are the better. If you get too serious and judgmental or start to lecture, you will most likely lose your audience quickly. Humor, cheerfulness, and enthusiasm help kids to open up.

Listen also to the music of the younger generation. It's likely when you were growing up, most teens enjoyed the same style of music. This is not the case today. The teen culture has a variety of favorite music styles, from rap and hip-hop to heavy metal. Whatever the style, music and musicians continue to be a strong influence in the lives of teenagers, meeting three basic needs:

1. Musicians (via CD, iPod, iTunes, radio, and video) spend huge amounts of time with young people—providing **companionship.**

2. Musicians accept young people as they are—providing **acceptance.**

3. Musicians often relate to the young person's problems—providing **identification.**

It is parents who should be providing companionship, acceptance, and identification. When we fail, our kids fill the void with something or someone else.

AN EYE-OPENING CONCERT EXPERIENCE

In the middle of writing this book I had to travel to the beautiful island of Oahu to speak at a marriage conference. (I couldn't get anyone to feel sorry for me.) My wife didn't want to miss an important baby shower, so my youngest daughter, Heidi, made the trip with me. Saturday night, after speaking all day, we had tickets to attend a Jack Johnson concert at the Waikiki Shell. Ziggy Marley was also performing. The outdoor concert had been sold out for a month and was the talk of Honolulu. We had received complimentary tickets, and I think I could have scalped the seats for the price of my airfare to Hawaii. As a culture watcher, I was so glad to be there. People sang with all the songs and danced most of the evening. From stage to audience, it seemed like friends just having a good time together. Alcohol was flowing, and in our section some people were sharing their marijuana with others they probably just met. As I said, what a place to watch culture.

I just kept thinking, *What is it that excites these people so much?* As I watched and listened, I realized the concertgoers felt a connection with the performers and songs. What was important to Jack and Ziggy seemed important to the fans. Jack, a native of Hawaii, asked everyone to clean up their beer cups and pizza cartons before they left. He mentioned that after his concert the previous year, he got a letter from the city saying the grounds were left absolutely spotless. At one point, Ziggy brought his mother and two of his young children on stage. The whole night felt like a family reunion, fans included. From the stage I heard absolutely nothing raunchy or crass like I have heard at other concerts. Once again I was reminded of the huge influence of musicians, as well as actors and other celebrities. Most would never claim to be role models for this generation, but they are, and we see it in how our kids talk and act and even in what they wear.

Culture expert Walt Mueller, in his article "5 Truths About Pop Culture," says *pop culture is market driven*. This generation of kids is the most aggressively targeted segment in the world today. They have the most disposable income. Marketers spend millions and millions of dollars studying teens, trying to connect with them and influence their shopping habits. Mueller talks about how *pop culture is fluid*. Because culture is trying to grab the attention of kids, it is constantly reinventing itself. People are looking for what is edgy, new, and exciting when it comes to style, music, ideas, and icons. Mueller says *pop culture is pervasive*. The culture is everywhere, it's inescapable. Pop culture has touched and shaped virtually all social institutions, including schools, churches, homes, and community. Mueller also goes on to say that *pop culture is entertaining and unifying*. Let's face it, it must get the attention of kids in order to survive, and it has to be relational because teens yearn for connection. Pop culture binds children and teens together in the strongest of ways.[2]

WHAT CAN A PARENT DO?

Taking a walk in the teen culture can get pretty interesting as well as cause deep concern, but with the right attitude, it doesn't have to. It does take more energy and time to help this generation of young people. Teens are growing up in an amoral culture. This is somewhat of a new phenomenon. In generations past, the biblical worldview was the accepted standard. Not everyone followed it, but if they deviated from it, they recognized they had done something wrong. That's not the case today. However, we can't give up and we can't back down. We can make a difference when we are proactive.

Set Parental Standards

When it comes to culture, as well as building morals and values into the lives of your kids, what are the absolutes? You can't make everything a fight, but teens who become healthy, responsible adults often say that they understood their parents' expectations. They received expressed expectations about behavior, and they knew the consequences ahead of time. Parents can promote restraint and teach their children a biblical worldview. Your teens can rebel, or even experiment with unwise behavior, but still they must know your boundaries and your standards. Frankly, most kids really do want to please their parents even if they don't always act like it.

Teens can rebel, or even experiment with unwise behavior, but still they must know your boundaries and your standards.

Teach Your Kids to Learn to Discern

It is better to teach your teen how to discern culture's impact than to keep him or her in a bubble. When kids are younger, parents must truly protect their children from unhealthy cultural influences, but as they become teenagers, a different parenting style is needed, much more like a coaching relationship. My kids would say Cathy and I were quite strict on media intake, but at the same time, we let them see certain movies as long as we went along and all of us could dialog after the movie. If you keep your teens in a bubble, that bubble will burst when they get out of the house with more freedom. So create an atmosphere of dialog, not just parental monolog. You can't fake dialog just to get your points across either. You will truly need to listen to your kids' opinions. As parents we can agree to disagree, but we must honor our kids by valuing their opinions and giving them the tools to learn to discern what culture is throwing at them. We just have to keep in mind that we are trying to develop responsible adults who will need decision-making tools when they live on their own.

Use Experiential Learning to Help Change Their Lives

It's clear the teenage years are an experimental period. They may move away from authority figures and think they are invincible. "It won't happen to me" is often their cry as they experiment with extreme behaviors.

Use this experimental phase and direct it toward positive experiences.

My advice is to use this experimental phase and direct it toward positive experiences. For example, I remember a father sitting with me and telling me how self-centered his son had become. He was lazy and had a bad attitude. The dad was at his wits' end. I suggested he take his son on a mission and service project in Mexico sponsored by our church. Men were needed to go with some students to help build an orphanage. They would have to sleep on a hard cement floor. The food would be lousy, and they wouldn't take a shower for a week. The son was hardly enthusiastic about the trip, but his dad signed them up anyway.

The dad called me after the experience and talked about seeing an almost miraculous transformation in his son. The trip seemed to throw off the boy's equilibrium. He worked hard, played with the poor children in the village, was engaged with the church services, and bonded with his dad in a way that had not happened in a long time. I could tell in the dad's voice that he was beaming; he felt like he had his son back. Of course, one mission experience won't always change someone's attitude, but this kid needed to get away from his environment and experience something extremely different. It moved him and he responded. By the way, today that young man works with a relief organization making a difference in the world in a wonderful way. Give your kids experiences that stretch and challenge them. And it's not a bad opportunity for you to go right along with them.

Encourage Positive Peer Influence

One theme in any good book on teens is the powerful influence of friends. Back in chapter 1, I talked a bit about how peer pressure isn't always negative. Peers can have a positive influence. The Bible says "bad company corrupts good character" (1 Corinthians 15:33), but the opposite is also true: Good company encourages good character.

Healthy friendships will help your teen deal with unhealthy cultural influences. So do everything you can to know your teen's friends and to help foster positive activities at school, church, and elsewhere. All studies show that young people who are engaged with positive activities and a positive school environment tend to have much more strength to overcome the negative cultural temptations. This is why I love church youth groups. They provide a fun, spiritually strong environment with healthy role models and the opportunity for quality friendships.

Today as I write this chapter, one of my very best boyhood friends, Terry Terrell, died of cancer. We had been Little League buddies and played sports together in high school. During our senior year over the Christmas holiday, I brought Terry to a Christian retreat where he made the most important decision of his life—to become a Christ follower. That one youth ministry experience determined much of the rest of his life on earth and his eternal relationship with God. His friendships, vocation, marriage, children, and so much of his life were centered around the courageous decision Terry made on New Year's Eve with his best friends by his side.

Foster Spiritual Growth

Studies show that kids who develop their own spiritual disciplines and stay involved in the church are much less vulnerable to at-risk behaviors. This makes for a challenge, though, because the teen years are often when they question their faith or drift from church. You can't live out a spiritual life for your teen, and nagging them into a deeper relationship with God has never worked, *ever*. However, building a home environment that fosters spiritual growth and gives your kids plenty of opportunities to mature will definitely enhance their ability to apply their own faith to the culture. Don't give up on them. Teens can be extremely committed to developing and nurturing their spiritual life. It just may look different than yours.

The Power of Being There

No matter what your teen says or acts like, your presence in his or her life makes a difference. Children young and old regard our very presence as a sign of caring and connectedness. I call this the power of being there. And in the midst of an unstable society and the chaos that tends to come with the teenage years, there is nothing stronger than the presence of a loving, nurturing, fun-loving parent who is willing to just "be there" for their kids. Don't expect much in return, but know that it does make a difference.

No matter what your teen says or acts like, your presence in his or her life makes a difference.

Looking back on the teen years of my own kids, they weren't easy and I didn't get as many hugs and kind words from them as when they were younger, but now that they are in their twenties, they are beginning to give me hints that they appreciated my presence back then. So persevere and continue to be a healthy presence in the lives of your teens. You are their insurance policy that they will be loved no matter what they do and how they act. No one said it would be easy. But it is worth it.

PART TWO

Common Problems and Solutions

EATING DISORDERS

One of the most common problems affecting teens, especially girls, is eating disorders. Perhaps surprisingly, anorexia, bulimia, and other eating disorders are often affiliated with good kids. These are not the teens who are using drugs and alcohol or even sex to medicate their pain. These are usually the kids who are getting excellent grades and truly want to please their parents.

So much about eating disorders is related to body image. Today's pop culture encourages girls and guys to live up to a slim body type that most people can't attain. Our culture often talks about obesity and weight gain as a problem; yet there are over ten million women and one million men suffering from either bulimia (binging and purging) or anorexia nervosa (a deep fear of gaining weight). Both bulimia and anorexia can be life threatening, and parents must take these issues seriously.

An *eating disorder* is a term used by medical professionals to describe a person's obsession with food, weight, or inappropriate eating behavior. Anorexia is often regarded as an emotional disorder involving self-starvation that produces a very thin body and leads to heart problems, osteoporosis, changes to the brain, and other health problems. Bulimia is generally a pattern of binging and then purging food, either through self-induced vomiting or the use of laxatives and diuretics. Bulimia can be very addictive and cause many health risks as well.

Take the time to become aware of the symptoms of anorexia and bulimia. The following lists are not complete, but if you notice that your child has even a few of these symptoms, seek help immediately from a professional.

Symptoms of Anorexia Nervosa

- Dramatic weight loss with no evident physical illness
- Excessive exercise
- Preoccupation with food, calories, nutrition, or cooking
- Feeling "fat" when not obese
- Refusal to eat or eating only small amounts
- Loss of menstrual period
- Thinness to the point of emaciation
- Distorted body image
- Strange obsession with food rituals
- Frequent weighing
- Perfectionism

Symptoms of Bulimia

- Binging and purging food
- Overeating and then spending an extreme amount of time in the bathroom
- Secretive about food and disappearing to the bathroom after a meal
- Feeling out of control
- Emotional instability or impulsivity
- Depression and mood swings
- Dental problems
- Feeling guilty about eating, with an obsessive focus on weight and body image

Parents can't move into denial when it comes to eating disorders. You are not your teen's best friend; you are his or her parent. So if you sense a problem, take action. It is better to be safe than sorry.

DRUG AND ALCOHOL USE AND ABUSE

Most teenagers will experiment with drugs and alcohol. This doesn't mean they are bad or will become addicts, but the experimental behavior that occurs at adolescence can quickly bring problems to a family, some deadly. The Franklin family lost their son as the result of a drunk driving incident. It was the first time their son, the school's quarterback and a leader of their church's youth group, tried driving after a few beers. Another set of parents is still dealing with fallout from their daughter's drug use. Jasmine says it started because everyone else at school was trying marijuana. She smoked a joint because of peer influence, but liked it so much she couldn't stop. She ended up in rehab and has brought other problems with her.

No matter what your family is like, drugs and alcohol are at your child's doorstep. In this brief section, I can't talk about all the issues, but let me address a few. To start with, parents must become aware of what are called gateway drugs—substances that often lead to more dangerous drug use. The gateway to abuse is wide and attractive at a young age with this generation of teens. There are at least four components:

Beer and wine. This is where most kids begin. They find the beer and wine in their home or their friends' homes. The average first drink of alcohol occurs at age twelve. If they continue the habit, it is very possible they will move through the gateway and experiment with the next gateway drug.

Nicotine. Nicotine is one of the stronger addictive drugs known to humankind. In the United States, the only population group where smoking is growing is with teens and young adults. Many girls have found that smoking helps them lose weight. If a person smokes cigarettes there is an 80 percent chance they will move to the next gateway and try marijuana. If a teen doesn't try cigarettes, there is only a 20 percent chance that they will ever smoke marijuana.

Marijuana and harder alcohol. The marijuana consumed today is five to twenty times stronger than the marijuana of previous generations, and it is often laced with other drugs. Marijuana is known to produce amotivational syndrome, which means the brain becomes lazy and lethargic. And like alcohol's effect, marijuana leaves you unable to make good decisions. Harder alcohol (stronger than beer and wine) is considered a gateway drug because alcohol is a mood- and mind-altering substance. What many people don't understand is that there is a biological predisposition toward alcoholism. If alcoholism is in your family system, there is a greater chance you can become an alcoholic. Because alcoholism is prevalent in my family system, I choose not to drink and have made sure my children understand about their increased risk of alcoholism too. I taught them that all alcoholics have a high tolerance for alcohol. Compared with others, they can actually drink more alcohol and not be drunk as quickly. Marijuana and harder alcohol use makes it easier to move to the next gateway.

Harder drugs. Kids today are experimenting with all types of even more dangerous drugs. The following is not meant to be all-inclusive, but parents must become aware of the different drugs teens are using:

- *Club drugs* are popular at teen parties. Club drugs tend to be stimulants and even psychedelic drugs. Examples include ecstasy, Rohypnol, and ketamine.

- *Hallucinogens* distort a person's sense of perception of reality. Examples include PCP, LSD, and mescaline.

- *Inhalants* are substances that people often don't consider drugs at first glance. However, they are considered addictive, and kids use them to get high. Spray paint, hair spray, and even vegetable oil sprays are some of the inhalants used today.

- *Prescription drugs*, of course, are found in many homes' medicine cabinets. Today, kids will try "pharming" at parties by experimenting with someone else's prescription drugs, including Ritalin, OxyContin, and Vicodin.

- *Cocaine, meth,* and *heroin* are three of the most popular drugs with teens when they move on to the stronger stuff. If your teen is experimenting with any of these dangerous substances, do everything in your power to get him the help he needs before it is too late.

Identifying the Warning Signs of Drug Abuse

With teenagers, it's not always easy to tell if they are in a crisis or just having a bad day. If you suspect your teenager is having trouble with alcohol or drugs, it's important that you take a closer look to help determine the causes of your suspicions. What you find may reveal that your teenager is simply on the rocky road of adolescence. On the other hand, you may find that your son or daughter needs significant help.

Subtle Symptoms of Chemical Abuse

The following symptoms could point to problems other than drug abuse. But they all indicate problems needing professional treatment. If every symptom describes your child, immediate action should be taken. If only a few symptoms are present, they could be common aspects of the teenage years. I suggest that you at least discuss your concerns with your child.

- Secrecy
- Changes in friends
- Increased isolation
- Change in interests or activities
- Drop in grades
- Getting fired from an after-school job
- Changes in behavior around the home
- Staying out all night
- Possession of a bottle of eye drops (to counter bloodshot eyes)
- Sudden change in diet that includes sweets and junk food (many drugs give users cravings or "the munchies")
- Dropping out of sports participation

Not-So-Subtle Symptoms of Chemical Abuse
The following symptoms indicate chemical abuse. If several of these symptoms are present in your child, you should take action immediately before the problem develops into addiction.

- Deep depression accompanied by hours of extra sleep
- Depression
- Extreme withdrawal from the family

- Increased, unexplained absenteeism from school
- Little or no involvement in church activities
- Increase in mysterious phone calls that produce a frantic reaction
- Starting smoking
- Money problems
- Extreme weight loss or gain
- Appearance of new friends, older than your child
- Expulsion from school
- Rebellious and argumentative behavior
- Listening to heavy-metal rock or rap music with pro-drug lyrics
- Acting disconnected or spacey
- Physically hurting younger siblings
- Attempting to change the subject or skirt the issue when asked about drug or alcohol use
- Changing the word *party* from a noun to a verb
- Discussing times in the future when he or she will be allowed to drink legally
- Long periods spent in the bathroom
- Burnt holes in clothes or furniture

Surefire Indicators of Chemical Abuse

When the following signs are noticeable, you should have no question in your mind that your child is abusing drugs or alcohol. These are signals that the problem has not just started but has existed for some time. Intervention is necessary if the following symptoms surface.

- Drug paraphernalia found in the bedroom
- Possession of large amounts of money (usually indicates selling drugs in addition to using)
- Needle marks on the arms, or wearing clothing that prevents you from seeing the arms
- Valuables disappearing from the house
- Arrests due to alcohol- or drug-related incidents
- Repeated bloodshot eyes
- Uncontrollable bursts of laughter with no apparent reason
- A runny or itchy nose that is not attributable to allergies or a cold (a red nose would also be an indicator)
- Dilated or pinpoint pupils
- Puffy or droopy eyelids that partially hang over the iris
- Mention of suicide or an attempt at suicide
- Disappearance or dilution of bottles in the liquor cabinet
- Time spent with people you know use drugs or alcohol
- Medicine disappearing from the medicine cabinet
- Defending peers' right to use drugs or alcohol

TATTOOS AND BODY PIERCING

There's no doubt about it, tattoos and body piercings are as big in today's youth culture as long hair and funky clothing were in the hippie culture of the 1960s and 1970s. As I have said before, a normal part of adolescence is wanting to become independent (and different!) from their parents. While we still see this happen in the area of clothes and hairstyles, piercings and tattoos have become part of today's fashion scene. As a result, it is not abnormal for your kids to be interested in these things. However, an adolescent's desire for tattoos and piercings (which are much more permanent than a change in hairstyle) may leave you uncomfortable.

So how do we, as parents, handle the issue? Unfortunately, there are no easy answers. Here are some comments and issues to consider when trying to decide if tattoos and piercings are right for your kids.

As a parent, you are in the position of authority (which is probably obvious—though not always an easy thing or evident with a teenager). You have to make the call on this. One of the most common tips for parenting adolescents is to choose your battles wisely. Personally, Cathy and I decided to tell our children that while they were under our roof and reliant on our finances, we did not want them to get tattoos. What they do as adults when they are on their own is up to them. We told them tattoos were an art form and some art goes out of style. If they wanted a tattoo as an adult, we suggested they get the tattoo art drawn on a piece of paper and carry it around for at least a year. If they still wanted it, then they would have a better understanding of what was going to be a permanent work of art on their body. Piercing of ears—no problem, but if anywhere else, not without our permission while they were teenagers.

A team of researchers from the Rochester School of Medicine and the Naval Medical Center in San Diego found that teens with tattoos and body piercings are more likely to be involved in at-risk behaviors, including increased sexual activity, drug/alcohol usage, eating disorders, and suicide.[1]

The American Dental Association opposes oral (tongue, lip, or cheek) piercing and calls it a public health hazard. The American Academy of Dermatology has taken a position against all forms of body piercing with one exception: the ear lobe (they also don't object as strenuously to belly button piercing). Further, both the U.S. and Canadian Red Cross won't accept blood donations from anyone who has had a body piercing or tattoo within a year because both procedures can transmit dangerous blood-borne diseases. Also, piercing body parts includes risks such as chronic infection, prolonged bleeding, scarring, hepatitis B and C, tetanus (lockjaw), abscesses or boils, permanent holes in nostril or eyebrow, chipped or broken teeth, and speech impediments.

You will want to be sure to talk about the following factors, but don't always expect your teens to agree with your opinion:

- *Passing fads*. Remind your teen about other fads and trends that are no longer in style.

- *Appearance*. Ask your teen how he wants to be viewed by other people.

- *Health concerns.* It takes a long time for the body to heal from a piercing.
- *Compromise.* If you can't stand the thought of your child with a tongue bar or a tattoo, come up with a solution you can both agree on.

COPING WITH TRAGEDY

Our kids are growing up with instant exposure to school shootings, hurricanes, earthquakes, and other tragedies. These tragedies are devastating not only to those involved but to people all around the world who are watching and feeling the pain and loss, often up close and personal thanks to global TV and the Internet. The sights and sounds of devastation can easily create a feeling of being overwhelmed for you and your teen.

Parents can play a vital role in helping their kids cope with the overwhelming tragedy associated with these crises. To help you help your kids, I've put together some ideas that you might find helpful.

- *Be willing to discuss natural disasters and tragedies with your kids.* Children, particularly younger ones, can be scared by tragedies and wonder if something similar could happen to them. Ask them whether they have been thinking about the crisis. Find out if news of the disaster has made them afraid. Talk with them and especially take time to listen, even if their fears seem unreasonable. Remember, a crisis is always self-defined. Answer their questions and share with them your concerns.

- *Tell them the truth.* Honesty is always the best policy, but that doesn't mean you need to share every gruesome detail of a devastation with your kids. Young teens can be frightened by such cold, hard facts, so be sure to be age-appropriate when talking to your kids about any disaster.

- *Shelter your younger teens and preteens from graphic video and pictures.* With 24/7 live news coverage from around the world, be aware that any disturbing video and pictures don't have to be part of conveying the "news" of what's happening to your children. My advice is that when natural disasters strike—especially in the immediate aftermath—keep the television news programs off when your younger kids are around.

- *Reassure your kids as best you can.* Since you don't have control over natural disasters like tsunamis, hurricanes, earthquakes, or other disasters that your own regions might be vulnerable to, as parents, you shouldn't promise a child that you will protect them from any harm that a catastrophe may bring. Your job here is to reassure them as best you can. If kids are worried about something bad occurring, tell them how unlikely it is to happen. And, of course, you can tell them, "We will do everything we can to always make sure you are safe from harm."

- *Don't ignore the spiritual issues.* If you've ever wondered about what your kids think about God, you'll probably find out in the wake of a disaster. Be prepared for questions like "Why did God let so many people die?" Sometimes it takes a crisis to bring those questions to the forefront. And if you don't have all of the answers, that's okay. Work to help your kids (and maybe even yourself) search for the answers.

- *Pray for people who have been impacted by the disaster.* If your family doesn't have a regular family prayer time, I encourage you to start one. Praying as a family for people affected by a tragedy also reinforces with your kids your own belief in God's love and His power to care and heal those who have been hurt.

- *Give.* As a family, find a way to give something—anything—to help people in need. Giving to those in need is a spiritual response. The call of Christ is a call to serve. Giving helps your kids learn to cope with tragedy by serving and helping those in need. Giving provides them a tangible way to respond. Your giving does not have to be limited to money. Typically, following a natural disaster, all kinds of supplies and food are needed to help the victims.

CYBERBULLYING

Through the Internet, e-mail, texting, and blogging, cyberspace has become part of the cultural landscape for adolescents today. Its negative effects, including cyberbullying, are becoming well-publicized. Authorities tell us that over 160,000 kids stay away from school in the United States every day because they are being bullied. Teens view cyberbullying as one of the new key problems in their culture. We parents didn't have to deal with this issue growing up, so we need to guard against being insensitive to what our kids face. My own children have had terrible cyberbullying experiences, including someone sending nude photos to one of our daughters and a young man writing an e-mail saying he would kill another daughter. Both times we chose to take the situations seriously and report them to local police authorities. It is vital that parents understand cyberbullying and then find ways to help protect children from its abuse.

What Is Cyberbullying?

Cyberbullying takes a variety of forms, but it commonly includes the use of negative, inappropriate, or threatening e-mail, instant messages, cell phone text messages, and posts to blogs or Web sites. Additionally, some cyberbullies pretend to be someone else and post online messages in order to cause trouble for the real person. Others pose as "friends" in order to coax personal information from an individual with the intent of broadcasting the information to others for the purpose of embarrassing or hurting that person.

Cyberbullying is extremely common. According to researchers at Clemson University, cyberbullying was experienced by 18 percent of the middle schoolers they surveyed. "Our statistics are conservative," said Clemson psychologist Robin Kowalski. "For every incident reported, many more go unreported."[2] Victims of cyberbullying often are the people who resort to it the most. Researchers reported that kids who are victimized "seem to be heavily involved in bullying others." The reason? While intimidation often prevents kids who have been physically bullied from retaliating physically, cyberbullying eliminates the intimidation factor. As a result, girls rule the cyberbullying world; guys still rule the bullying world on playgrounds and school hallways.[3]

How to Protect Your Kids From Cyberbullies

- Educate yourself and your kids about electronic communications. Take the time to learn about how e-mail, instant messaging, cell phone text messaging, and blogging works. Learn what security measures are available in these tools to help block unwanted and inappropriate messages from being delivered.

- Set ground rules with your family about electronic communications. Give kids clear guidelines on what constitutes acceptable and unacceptable electronic communication. Determine what kinds of personal information, if any, you deem to be acceptable for your kids to give out electronically. Have your kids agree to report to you any inappropriate communications they receive or find about themselves posted somewhere else. Setting standards for your expectations on how your kids communicate to others will help prevent your kids from becoming cyberbullies.

- Frequently search the Internet for your kids' names, e-mail addresses, screen names, etc., using multiple search engines (Google, Yahoo!, etc.). This will allow you to see what, if anything, is floating out in cyberspace about your kids. Also, be sure to search under "Images," "Groups," and other categories each search engine offers, which might turn up more electronic information about your kids. When you search, use quotation marks before and after your child's name, as in "John Doe"—otherwise you'll get results back on every Web site that has John or Doe in it.

- If your child receives or finds a negative message about him or her once, don't overreact. Any kid can become the object of a one-time prank. Keep your eye on the situation, but don't overreact unless the message threatens physical harm.

If your child becomes the target of repeated cyberbullying:

- Be sure to talk with your child. See if she knows or can guess who is responsible for the cyberbullying. Check with her to see how she is emotionally handling the abuse. Give support and provide help whenever needed. Reinforce your expectation that she is not to retaliate by becoming a cyberbully herself.

- If you are unable to identify the cyberbully, block the messages through your e-mail settings, instant message settings, or Internet service provider, if possible. If the negative messages are posted to a blog or Web site, report the abuse to the Web site's management. For example, if an inappropriate message is posted on the popular Web site MySpace, contact MySpace directly about the content of the message and where the message appears.

- Notify school officials. School officials are typically not able to address a cyberbullying situation that happens off campus. Still, they generally are familiar in dealing with the cyberbullying that happens on campus. Notification will alert them to keep an eye out for the situation on campus, and it's possible that they have insights into how to help your specific situation, particularly if they are currently dealing with the person or persons who are cyberbullying your child.

- If messages include physical threats, notify local law enforcement authorities. Don't delay. Print out a copy of the threatening material and take it with you to give to the authorities.

- When in doubt, report it! If you don't know what to do if your child is being cyberbullied, report it! Whether you report to the Internet service provider, Web site management, school authorities, or the police, most people will help point you in the right direction if they themselves aren't prepared or able to help you directly. What is likely is that if cyberbullying is not addressed, the abuse will continue, and this greatly raises the risk of your child reacting inappropriately.

In the end, like so many other issues of parenting, you set the pace when it comes to reacting to cyberbullies. Dealing with the issue calmly, intentionally, and in a God-honoring way sets an important example for your child.

DRIVING

Obtaining a driver's license is still one of the more anticipated rites of passage for teens, but it's increasingly apparent that driving is one of the most overlooked dangers our kids face. Many parents view their teen's driving years with mixed emotions. On the one hand, a driver's license signifies an end to the endless chauffeuring that is a hallmark of kids' younger years, and this brings some welcome relief to parents. On the other hand, teen driving leads to no shortage of anxiety about the dangers that come with inexperienced drivers.

How Parents Can Keep Teens Safe

While there is no guarantee your teen can avoid being involved in a motor vehicle accident while driving or while riding in a car being driven by another teen, you can help minimize the risks involved. Here's how:

1. *Be intentional.* Develop a plan for keeping your teen driver safe and implement it. Don't just assume that everything will work out okay without a plan in place. Don't put it off. Because the risks involved in teen driving are so daunting, being intentional about a plan is the only reasonable way to minimize the risks.

2. *Set clear expectations and consequences.* This is one area of parenting that your teen's safety, perhaps even their life, depends upon. Sit down with your teen and hash out the details together. Some areas for setting limits include:

- *Driving permission.* When will it be okay for your teen to drive? When will it not be okay? Late afternoon, evening, and night driving carry higher risks for teen drivers. Seek to minimize driving during these times as much as possible. Set standards for your teen riding along in other teen-driven vehicles as well.

- *Who can go along?* Many states use a graduated licensing system that prohibits and/or limits when teens can drive with other teenagers in the vehicle. Make sure you know your state's laws and ensure that they are followed. You might even choose to place your own tougher limits than the state requires.

- *Notification.* Do you want your teen to notify you before he gets behind the wheel? How about when he is going to ride in a vehicle driven by another teen? Do you want to be notified when your teen arrives at the destination? All of these issues should be considered and determined ahead of time.

- *Speeding.* Okay, obviously, you don't want your teen driver to speed. That's a given. But what will happen if they are caught violating the speed limit?

- *Cell phones.* Even if your state allows drivers to use cell phones, I suggest a policy of not allowing the use of a cell phone while driving. This means no receiving calls (even from you), no placing calls (even to you), and no checking or sending text messages. If your teen needs to use their cell phone in the case of an emergency, have them pull off the road to a safe location, park the car, and then use the cell phone.

- *Alcohol/drug usage.* This is another obvious "not allowed." Any violation should give rise to an appropriately severe consequence.

- *Seat belt usage.* No seatbelt, no drive, no exceptions. That is the best policy and in many states, the law.

3. *Practice, practice, practice.* Driving skills are improved through driving experience. Don't rush the process. The driver's license can wait awhile. Make sure you give your teen hours and hours (some experts suggest between fifty to one hundred hours over a six-month period) of practice driving that is supervised by you or another responsible adult.

Create a Car-Driving Contract

Teens need expressed expectations, and driving is no exception. On the next page is a sample contract I adapted from a "Dear Abby" column years ago.

Driving Contract

I, _____, agree to the following "rules of the road." If at anytime I violate this agreement, my driving privilege will be forfeited.

1. Traffic Tickets: I agree to pay all traffic violations on time and pay for any increase to my insurance premiums.

2. Accidents: If I am in an accident or do damage to the car, then I agree to pay for all damages not covered by insurance.

3. Drinking or Drug Use: At NO TIME will I ever drink alcohol or use drugs at the same time as driving. There will be no alcohol or drugs ever in the car. I will let no one in my car who has been drinking unless my parents have approved it.

4. Passengers: I will never allow more passengers in the car than there are seat belts for, and I will never allow a stranger in the car. I will not pick up hitchhikers.

5. Car cleanliness: Driving the car is a privilege and I will be responsible to keep the car clean as well as check the gas and oil regularly.

Signed,

_____   _____
Teen   Parents

CHOOSING A COLLEGE

A few weeks ago I was sitting next to a woman on a plane. I noticed she was diligently working through some college information brochures. "It looks like you have a child about ready to enter the college world," I said. She smiled and said, "Well, my daughter is only nine, but it's just never too early with all the pressure to get into the right schools." She left me a bit speechless because I do believe that early planning is a good thing for college finances, but kids or parents should not have the extra pressure to make sure they get everything just right when their child is in third grade. How soon should you start preparing for your child's college education? Talk to a thousand parents and you are bound to get a thousand different answers.

Cathy and I know what it's like to feel as though we didn't start saving soon enough for college expenses. If we had it to do over again, we would have started that process earlier. I have the privilege of being the senior director of the HomeWord Center at Azusa Pacific University, and I called upon my good friend Dr. Jon Wallace, the president of APU, to brainstorm with me on how to help your kids make the right decisions about college. Here is what we came up with:

- *Pray about it.* The college years are typically when a person makes some of the most important decisions in life— chief among them whether or not to marry and what kind of career path to pursue. These are decisions not made lightly, so it's important to bathe the college issue in prayer before deciding where and when to attend.

- *Ask others about their experiences.* Scripture reminds us "there is wisdom in the counsel of many." Do you know anyone who is already attending a school your teen is interested in? Get to know them. Ask them what it's like to attend the school they're attending. Practical experience will tell you more about a college or university than any handbook or brochure ever will.

- *Visit the campus.* This one might sound obvious, but you'd be amazed at the number of teens and their parents who make decisions about where to attend college based only on a brochure or a Web site. College is where your son or daughter will be spending some of the most foundational time of his or her life. Take a couple of days to visit, preferably when school is in session, and walk the campus. Sit in on a class or two. Talk to some of the professors and support staff. Really "try the place on."

- *Read everything you can about possible colleges.* This is another obvious point too many parents miss. Just because you have good memories from your days at "good old State U" doesn't mean a certain school will be right for your son or daughter. Get the brochures, surf the Internet, and both you and your teen do your homework!

- *Start saving now.* You know what they say, "There's no time like the present." This is especially true when it comes to saving for college. When I told Jon that Cathy and I didn't feel as though we started saving early enough for our daughters' college educations, he corrected me by reminding me that at least we had started. Whether your child is seventeen years old or seventeen months old, it's never too late (or too early) to start saving for college. Don't try to save the whole amount all at once. Save what you can and start doing it now.

- *Remember that grades do count.* High school can be a confusing time for young people. One moment, their main priority is getting straight As; the next, it's simply hanging out with friends and having a good time. Many scholarships are based on a student's GPA. So stress with your child the importance of earning good grades and maintaining a solid grade point average.

- *Search for scholarship help.* There are plenty of free scholarship search engines available online. It takes some time to search, but millions and millions of scholarship dollars are available. We asked our daughters to invest a few hours a week during their junior and senior years of high school. It's worth the investment of time.

- *Apply early to schools.* In many cases, institutional financial aid from a school is given to students who apply and are admitted early. For this reason, it is in everyone's best interest, both the student and his or her parents, to apply early! Some schools actually make the acceptance just a bit easier if you apply early also.

- *Meet deadlines!* Many times, state and federal government aid is contingent upon a student getting their FAFSA (Free Application for Federal Student Aid) in by a priority deadline. Families can start filling out the FAFSA for the upcoming school year as early as January 1 of that year.

DEPRESSION

A top concern of youth specialists in North America today is the rise in teen depression. Two million adolescents in the United States are classified as depressed, and over 60 percent of teens who are depressed are receiving no treatment for their situation.[4] Unfortunately, this is leading kids to learn to medicate their emotional pain with drugs and causing suicide to rise dramatically among adolescents. Parents must take all teen depression seriously. If you have any questions or concerns about your child's mental and emotional health, seek the help you need to get the right advice.

There are different types of depression among young people and adults. To get a good diagnosis early is always helpful. Your teen may have reactive depression, which is a common form of a mood problem, which tends to be the least serious. Bipolar depression, on the other hand, which is characterized as "manic depression" with huge mood swings, is more serious. Your job is not to place yourself as the physician or therapist. Rather, your job is to seek the right help for your child. The following are signs of depression for children and teenagers. The behavior of depressed kids can be different from what depressed adults exhibit.

Signs of Depression[5]

- Decreased interest in activities, or inability to enjoy favorite activities
- Frequent absences from school or poor performance in school
- Frequent sadness, tearfulness, crying
- Persistent boredom; low energy

- Low self-esteem and guilt
- Hopelessness
- Poor concentration
- Difficulty with relationships
- Social isolation, poor communication
- Increased irritability, anger, or hostility
- Talk of or efforts to run away from home
- Extreme sensitivity to rejection or failure
- A major change in eating and/or sleeping patterns
- Thoughts or expressions of suicide or self-destructive behavior
- Frequent complaints of physical illness such as headaches and stomachaches

Obviously, any of these signs and symptoms could mean something other than depression, but it is better to get an assessment from a professionally trained person.

DINNERTIME

There is overwhelming evidence that families who take the time to eat together regularly will have kids who are much less at risk for bad behaviors and more prone to getting good grades with healthier self-images. Many families are now making mealtime family time. Here are eight reasons why this is a great idea.

1. Kids who live in families that eat dinner together regularly are less likely to be involved in at-risk behaviors. A 2009 study found that children who eat dinner with their families infrequently (fewer than three times a week) are twice as likely to use tobacco or marijuana and more than one and a half times likelier to have used alcohol than teens who have five to seven family dinners a week.[6]

2. Families who eat dinner together regularly are more likely to have stronger, happier family relationships. As families struggle to find amounts of quantity and quality time together, family dinnertime provides the opportunity for both. Teens who frequently eat dinner with their family are likelier to say they have excellent relationships with their parents, and teens who have infrequent family dinners are likelier to say they have fair or poor relationships with their parents. When families hang out together and communicate, they grow strong and healthy.

3. Kids who live in families that eat dinner regularly together perform better in school. According to the latest research, compared to teens who have frequent family dinners, teens who have fewer than three

194

family dinners per week are one and a half times likelier to report getting mostly C's or lower grades in school.

4. Families who eat dinner together regularly develop a stronger family identity. Additionally, this family routine establishes a sense of stability and security that provides kids with a positive environment where they can grow into healthy adults.

5. Families who eat dinner together regularly can keep in touch with each other's lives. Everyone—kids and parents alike—can keep up to date during family dinnertime on what is going on with school, jobs, family life, and friends.

6. A regular family dinnertime provides natural opportunities for planning and problem solving. Scheduling family meeting times to discuss these things can be difficult. A regular family mealtime can offer a natural solution to the challenge.

7. Eating dinner regularly fosters learning. When families who eat dinner together engage in a variety of conversation topics, learning is encouraged. Kids who are exposed to regular family discussion times learn a broader vocabulary.

8. Kids are likely to receive better nutrition when eating dinner regularly with their families. A simple but true rule applies: When kids eat with their families, they eat better. A family dinnertime means kids are more likely to eat a nutritionally balanced meal that is lower in sugar and fat content than if they prepare or purchase meals on their own.

Some might shy away from regular family dinners due to the busy pace of life and concern for the amount of time a family meal requires. But the latest research shows that the average family meal lasts just thirty-five minutes. That's not a lot of time, but every minute can lead to some great benefits for your family!

OVERWEIGHT TEENS

According to the latest Centers for Disease Control reports, 67 percent of adults in the United States are overweight. In this society of inactivity and processed food, it's not a surprise that people struggle with weight issues. If your teen is overweight, for their health's sake, take action. I don't want to move from writing to meddling, but if you are overweight, you may need to do something about your own habits before you ask anything from your teen.

Overweight and obesity are complicated issues. Some kids have a family predisposition to being overweight, and others use comfort foods as a way of coping with their problems. Regardless of the situation, an overweight teen is often not a healthy teen, or they are on the road to more physical and emotional problems down the road in adulthood. Just like so many other aspects of raising healthy teens, you will have to set the pace. Good diet and exercise are always worth the pain. It's the pain of discipline or the pain of regret. Here are some helpful tips to consider in helping an overweight teen.

- *Exercise is the answer.* Experts recommend that kids on most, if not all, days get sixty minutes of moderate physical activity. Don't allow your teens to veg in front of the television or computer if they haven't had enough exercise. Make it fun for them, and if you can, join them for some good old-fashioned family bonding. You will have to set a good example. Kids watch what their parents do, and if the parents are pretty much couch potatoes, they will have a harder time encouraging their kids to exercise.

- *See that your teen gets a physical on a regular basis.* Kids grow at different rates. Your child's doctor can determine if your child is overweight or just waiting for a growth spurt to correct what may seem to be a weight issue.

- *Make good nutrition an all-family strategy.* Don't just try to help your overweight child eat more nutritious meals and portions. Again, role modeling is important. Involve the whole family. And don't put your teen on a diet unless your teen's physician suggests it. Good eating and proper exercise will take care of most overweight issues.

- *Teach alternative coping skills.* If your child uses eating as a coping mechanism to deal with problems, be sure that you get involved in teaching other more positive coping strategies.

- *Make sure your teen eats breakfast.* We've probably all heard the concept that breakfast is the most important meal of the day. For kids, this is especially true. Breakfast "sets the table" for your children, providing them with the energy they need to listen, learn, and be active in their school experiences.

- *Offer your child a wide variety of healthy foods.* Make sure that your teen has well-balanced nutrition, including grains, vegetables, fruit, low-fat dairy products, and other low-fat sources of protein, such as lean meats and beans. Pay attention to fat. These days nutritionists are concerned not only with the amount of fat but the types of fat. Smart parents are cooking with less fat.

- *Try to limit your teen's sugar intake.* Keep an eye on the amount of sugar your child is eating. Many prepared foods have too much sugar. Watch especially the amount of sugar your child is consuming through sugar-sweetened sodas and fruit drinks. One authority on teen weight issues told me, "Parents should be more concerned about their children's sugar addictions than drugs. More deaths are caused in our lifetime from poor eating habits than drug use."

SELF-INJURY

Seventeen-year-old Lauren was despondent over break-ing up with her boyfriend. She had never known pain so deep and lingering. She tried to drown her sorrows in her favorite activities, but nothing seemed to work. Even a trip to the movies turned sour when she noticed her former boyfriend with his new girl, watching the same film. Trying to keep her composure but hurting just the same, she inadvertently yanked the tab off her soda can. Without much thought, she pressed its sharp edge deep into the flesh of her thumb. The pain and the blood that followed unleashed what had been pent up inside of her since the relationship ended. But it also gave her something she had longed for all her life: a sense of control over her pain.

Within weeks, Lauren became a full-fledged self-injurer, or "cutter." She joined several million people in the United States who regularly injure themselves as a way of dealing with the deep pain in their lives. Cutting is most common, but other forms of self-injury include burning, bone breaking, and hair pulling. As you might imagine, self-injurers don't always come from stable, loving homes. It's estimated that about 50 percent have a history of physical or sexual abuse. One teenager said the physical pain she inflicted on herself helped her forget the pain of a childhood marred by sexual abuse.

In recent years, made-for-TV movies and popular televi-sion dramas about self-injury have brought this phenomenon to light. And in most, if not all of these story lines, the self-injurers were women. But in reality, just over 70 percent are women, most of them ranging in age from 11 to 26. The practice of self-injury and especially cutting has become almost mainstream, and some experts say it has reached "fad" status. Recently a group of middle school girls had all talked about cutting themselves at an overnight party. They did, but the behavior continued and quickly became out of control for the majority of the girls involved. Like so many other destructive behaviors, cutting is very prevalent among kids who grow up in Christian homes.

What's the appeal? Cutting is, at its core, an unhealthy act of coping. Only sometimes is it associated with suicidal thoughts; rather, it's a means of actually feeling something. Many teens who self-injure themselves say they felt numbness in their life and the cutting helped them deal with the pain. It is a physical act with an emotional release. Beyond the emotional release, the act of self-injury gives a sense of control as well as a physical satisfaction, as doctors note that cutting releases pleasurable endorphins.

Warning signs of self-injury include

- Unexplained and frequent scratches, burns, or cuts
- Scarring
- Attempts to conceal arms and legs with clothing (long sleeves and pants), even in hot weather
- Possession of numerous sharp objects
- Increased time spent alone

Self-injury behaviors typically begin during puberty. They often last for five to ten years but can persist much longer without appropriate treatment.

If you suspect your teen has been self-injuring, seek help from a mental health professional with self-injury expertise.[7]

SLEEP

Only about 8 percent of teens get adequate sleep. This can affect the physical and psychological health of teens as well as cause them to be more vulnerable to poor decision-making. Lack of sleep is rapidly becoming a major adolescent development problem. One third of teens report falling asleep in school twice a day![8] Poor sleep is linked to high blood pressure among teens. Teens with later bedtimes are more likely to become depressed and will tend to do more poorly in school. Many experts say it is time for parents to step in and help their children get more hours of sleep. A minimum of eight to nine hours of sleep a night is what is needed.

Technology and caffeine are keeping teens awake. Just one of five teens is getting the recommended eight hours of sleep each night. The rest may be texting the night away with the help of highly caffeinated energy drinks. Just like their parents, this generation of young people multitask into the night, and it is affecting their sleeping habits dramatically. Parents must reinforce the need for healthy sleeping habits and may have to pull the amount of accessible technology available in their teenager's bedroom. A majority of teens have a computer, TV, cell phone, and music device in their room, and too many times these devices are not monitored. My personal suggestion is to remove the computer and TV from the room. The cell phone must be placed in a charging device in the kitchen or other room at a certain time, and if the music device becomes a problem, then that becomes a "use privilege" as well.

Earlier bedtimes will decrease at-risk behaviors, decrease depression, and increase school success. With earlier bedtimes, kids may move back to enjoying reading and slowing down the pace. Unfortunately parents are not modeling healthy sleeping habits either. Teens that don't get adequate rest will tend to become adults who live the same way.[9]

SEXUAL ABUSE

Sexual abuse is a serious concern and problem in North America and all around the world. In the United States, one out of three young women will be sexually abused before they become an adult. For men, one out of five to six men are sexually abused before adulthood. Every day in this country, children and youth are being tricked, seduced, intimidated, and forced into sexual activity with another person. So what can parents do to prevent child sexual abuse?

- *Learn as much information as you can about physical and sexual abuse.* Learn who is most likely to commit crimes of abuse and why adults abuse kids, and discuss with your loved ones if you have any concerns. There are lots of Web sites that have preventative information about child sexual abuse. A simple search will turn up many of these resources.[10]

- *Listen and talk with your teens.* Good communication is the most important principle in keeping your kids safe from sexual abuse. Work to create a climate in your home where kids aren't afraid to share information about things they may be embarrassed about or afraid of. Be willing to share with your kids what you know about sexual abuse and how to prevent it. For instance, be sure to share with your kids basic information like, "No one has the right to touch your body without your permission."

- *Teach your kids personal safety rules and general information on sexual abuse.* Start early with your children (in an age-appropriate way) and set clear safety rules for your kids. Here is a list of safety rules to help you get started:

- Teach your kids the proper names for all their private parts; many children are not able to tell about the abuse because they don't know the words to use.

- Safety rules apply to all adults, not just strangers. (Eighty percent of sexual abuse is done by someone they know and often trust.)

- Nobody has the right to touch their body without their permission, regardless of how much he or she says they love them, how much money he or she has spent on them, or any other reason.

- Anytime a touch makes them feel uncomfortable, they have the right to say no. They never owe another person the right to touch them. Teach them to trust their gut feelings. Pushing, manipulating, pressuring, exploiting, or abusing another person is never acceptable in any relationship. Their bodies belong to them, and it is not okay for another person to touch their private parts.

- It is okay to say no if someone tries to touch their body or do things that make them feel uncomfortable, no matter who the person is. The same goes for showing photos or videos.

- If an adult or older teenager has touched them in the past, it is not their fault, and it is always the adult's responsibility.

- They should not keep secrets about touching, no matter what the person says; if someone touches them, tell and keep telling until someone listens!

- *Know the adults and teens in your children's lives.* From getting to know schoolteachers, coaches, and youth workers to interviewing potential babysitters, you should know as much as you can about the adults and teens your kids spend time with. If you have a cautionary feeling, don't let it pass. Follow through on your gut feelings.

- *Keep tabs on your kids.* As much as possible, know where your kids are and whom they are with. Make it a family rule that if your teens' plans change, they must notify you before they do something or go somewhere that you don't know about.

Victims of sexual abuse live in a world clouded by the fact that something very horrible has happened to them. They're devastated when it happens, but actually quite grateful to have someone to talk to about the abuse. That's why, if your son or daughter needs to talk, you can encourage them with these facts.

- *The abuse was not their fault.* It is always the fault of the abuser. Far too many young people blame themselves for the victimization that has taken place. Remove all fault from your child and remember this is not the time to lecture them.

- *It is good to talk out your feelings right now.* It's not healthy to suffer in silence. The natural tendency is to not tell anyone. The shame is so strong it keeps good kids from talking. But suffering in silence will never help them get better. The pain will continue to manifest in multiple ways in the young person's life. It's not easy to talk about the experience, but it is the road to healing and help.

- *There is hope and healing available.* After experiencing this kind of trauma, many young people lose hope, yet hope is what they need to move forward. I tell kids there are millions of people who have experienced what they have experienced, and those who are willing to seek help receive the healing they need. If you can find someone who has had a similar experience and found hope and healing through seeking help, that can help your teen in a big way.

- *Get counseling for sexual abuse now, in order to prevent problems as they grow older.* If they have never talked with a counselor, seek help immediately. This is not something a parent can handle on their own.

- *God cares. He really does!* Sexual abuse as much as any trauma brings about strong feelings of anger and questioning God. Let your child know that if Jesus wept at the death of a friend, then He weeps for your child's pain. He doesn't promise to take away all our sorrow, but He does promise to walk with us through our darkest moments.

Sometimes, just hearing these assurances from the person they trust most can be the starting point to recovery for a child who has been sexually abused.

SUICIDE

Suicide is the third leading cause of death among teenagers, and the incidence of teenage suicide has more than tripled over the last thirty years. Suicide is obviously a subject that no parent wants to ever face, but with today's growing concerns, it is vital to be aware of common issues and solutions to help your teen stay safe.

There are many myths about suicide, and sometimes even people in the helping professions hold common misunderstandings.

- *Myth #1: Suicide occurs without warning.* Actually, most suicidal people give multiple warnings. Parents tend to miss the warnings or dismiss them as "That's just our daughter's overreaction." Take every warning or sign seriously. Warning signs of a potential suicide are available from many trustworthy Web sites, including www.suicidology.org. Unfortunately, the ultimate warning is an attempted suicide, and as parents we want to do all we can not to get to that point.

- *Myth #2: People who talk about suicide won't do it.* The truth is, 80 percent of those who commit suicide did talk about it, but the people with whom they talked probably didn't take the warning seriously. Many parents are afraid of mentioning the word *suicide* because it may give their kids the idea. If you even suspect a child is considering suicide, ask him or her.

- *Myth #3: Suicidal people don't seek medical help.* Research shows that three out of four people visited a doctor for some reason within one to three months of the suicide.

- *Myth #4: All suicidal people are mentally ill.* Too many people believe that suicide only happens to people who are mentally ill. The fact is that only 15 percent of people who take their lives have actually been diagnosed as mentally ill. Most of the time people who are suicidal appear normal to those around them.

- *Myth #5: Suicidal people are totally committed to dying.* One of the most common characteristics of adolescents who are contemplating suicide is ambivalence. They have a strong desire to end their lives, but they also have a strong desire to live. You can give them hope and security, and that can easily change their mind. They are looking for a reason to live.

- *Myth #6: When the depression lifts, the suicide crisis is over.* Often the lifting of depression means the adolescent has finally decided to take his or her own life. Once the decision has been made, the depression is sometimes replaced with an almost manic attitude of euphoria.

My good friend Rich Van Pelt, an expert in the field, taught me years ago that what is needed for a teen to commit suicide is a *time, place,* and *method.* If a child has discussed a time, a place, and a method of killing himself, then take this extremely seriously. Seek help and don't delay. If there is a plan in place, the best way to stop it is to intervene, which usually means a complete evaluation at a hospital. If your child is suicidal, seek help immediately, and if they have discussed any suicidal method, make sure the means is taken away from them. Suicide is a permanent solution to a temporary problem. There are times when parents are just simply caught off guard. But regardless of the situation, a parent who is informed and seeks help will typically see the temporary problem go away.

Let me just admit upfront that Cathy and I struggled with homework issues as much as anyone. Our kids are extremely smart. We were motivated to help, coerce, bribe, shame, restrict, and do whatever it took to get them to college. It caused tension in our home and, at times, tension between us as a couple. A story I recently told on my radio broadcast basically describes our turmoil. I had to confess this story to John Rosemond, the author of the excellent book *Ending the Homework Hassle*.[11] When our daughter Christy was younger, we made her do her own science projects. The other kids in her class must have had dads and moms who were engineers, because their projects were amazing. Christy's was good for a fourth grader who did it on her own, but it was usually the worst in the class. Finally in sixth grade I took things into my own hands. Since I am mechanically and artistically challenged, I invited a friend of mine to help me with Christy's project. Christy was placed in a chair to watch this creation of art and science. It was a papier-mâché volcano with smoke coming from the inside. We worked and painted long after Christy went to bed. It looked pretty good, if I do say so myself.

The next day I took it to the classroom. I didn't trust Christy to carry it. That night at the school's open house, the teacher came right up to me and told me how much she appreciated that we allowed Christy to do her own work, because the other parents seemed to "take over." I was puzzled by the teacher's input. Then I saw Christy's project. The volcano had sunk. It was partly broken off and the smoke had burned a hole in the paper. Then I noticed Christy crying next to "my piece of work." I think I learned a lesson that day. My children's homework was their job, not mine. (Now that I think about it, I don't think I ever confessed to the teacher that I was the culprit. Here I am writing a parenting book, and I allowed my little daughter to take the fall on the broken volcano!)

During my "confessional" radio broadcast, John introduced the ABCs of ending the homework hassle. It's one of the most freeing ways to deal with homework, yet admittedly, it is difficult for anyone who is a control addict. These ABCs are nothing more than the approach to homework that parents used fifty years ago. Let me pass them along to you.

A: *All by Myself.* Teens ought to be responsible for doing their own homework. Find a private place for your teen to do their homework and help them set up an environment conducive to study. Then leave them alone. If they flunk the homework assignment, they chose the consequence. We have to teach them independence.

B: *Back Off.* What may be the most difficult step for many parents is to back off. This means to refuse to give your kids your constant attention at homework time. Nagging really doesn't work in the long run. Some would say it is like a constant dripping and a form of torture. John says about 80 percent of the time, "I need help" means they are looking for someone to fix a problem or bail them out. It's possible to back off from helping the kids do the homework and turn your role more into supporting and encouraging. Even if your teen fails the homework assignment, they will learn an important life lesson from the experience. Don't rob them of this learning experience.

C: *Call It Quits.* Many parents set a time when kids must begin their homework and a time for them to quit. Set deadlines to finish the work. John strongly advises, "When it's time to quit, it's time to quit." This gives your kids plenty of time to get it done, but it isn't a fight every night that ends up creating a very poor family environment. This will give your kids a chance to learn to manage time more effectively.

Remember, the goal is to raise self-reliant kids in a self-indulgent world. It takes as much discipline on the parent's part as it does the young people's. The result is worth the effort.

Sample Family Contracts and Agreements

SAMPLE INTERNET USAGE CONTRACT

The average amount of time I will spend online will be no more than _____ hours per day.

I will limit my Web surfing to educational, Christian, or other family-friendly sites only.

Unsolicited e-mails and forwards with attachments will be deleted unopened. Internet filters will be used at all times.

SAMPLE MUSIC AGREEMENT

The number of hours music can be played in the home is _____ per day/week. _____ are the only acceptable styles of music to be listened to anywhere (home, car, school, friend's house). I may not attend any concerts where _____ (names of groups) are playing.

SAMPLE TV/MOVIE VIEWING CONTRACT

The average amount of time the TV can be on in our home is _____ hours per day/week. Television programs with ratings of _____ are not acceptable in our home. _____ are not acceptable TV programs in our home. The only movie ratings that are available for each family member to view are _____. The family agreement about MTV (or VH1 or other channels) is _____.

An example of a TV program that could be a fun family weekly date is _____.

A movie that supports the biblical standards of our family is

_____.

About the Author

Jim Burns, PhD, founded the ministry HomeWord in 1985 with the goal of bringing help and hope to struggling families. Jim is host of the HomeWord radio broadcasts, heard daily in over eight hundred communities, and senior director of the HomeWord Center for Youth and Family at Azusa Pacific University. In addition to the radio program, Jim speaks to thousands around the world each year through seminars and conferences and is an award-winning author whose books include *Teaching Your Children Healthy Sexuality*, *The Purity Code*, and *Confident Parenting*. He has been featured through media outlets including CNN, ABC, and Focus on the Family. Jim and his wife, Cathy, have three grown daughters and live in Southern California. For more information, visit www.HomeWord.com.

Notes

Chapter 1: Who Is That Stranger in Your House?

1. For this and subsequent references to HomeWord radio broadcasts, visit the Audio section of our Web site, http://www.homeword.com.

2. One out of five students has received a text message with a sexual image on their cell phone. Often the image is of another kid from their school. Cox Communications, "Teen Online & Wireless Safety Survey: Cyberbullying, Sexting, and Parental Controls," Cox Communication, in Partnership with the National Center for Missing & Exploited Children and John Walsh, http://www.cox.com/takecharge/safe_teens_2009/media/2009_teen_survey_internet_and_wireless_safety.pdf (accessed August 3, 2010).

3. Anna Freud, "Adolescence," *The Writings of Anna Freud Volume V, 1957–1965* (New York: International Universities Press, 1969).

4. Walt Mueller, *The Space Between: A Parent's Guide to Teenage Development* (Grand Rapids, MI: Zondervan, 2009), 12.

5. Mark Holmen, *Faith Begins at Home* (Ventura, CA: Regal Books, 2005).

Chapter 2: Correcting Behavior Without Crushing Character

1. If you are looking for a parenting philosophy and model to look at, you may want to read my earlier book *Confident Parenting*.
2. Foster Cline, *Parenting Teens with Love and Logic* (Colorado Springs: Piñon Press, 2006), 139–140.
3. Jack Canfield and Mark Victor Hansen, *Chicken Soup for the Soul* (Deerfield Beach, FL: Health Communications, 1993), 266–267.

Chapter 3: Learning the Developmental Stages of Adolescence

1. Les Parrott, *Helping the Struggling Adolescent* (Grand Rapids, MI: Zondervan, 2000), 20.
2. Chap Clark and Dee Clark, *Disconnected: Parenting Teens in a MySpace World* (Grand Rapids, MI: Baker Books, 2007), 53–59.

Chapter 4: Creating a Media-Safe Home

1. HomeWord offers a free Weekly Culture Brief via e-mail that helps parents keep up with the latest culture and media trends. To subscribe, visit www.HomeWord.com.
2. Match.com and Chadwick Martin Bailey, "2009–2010 Studies: Recent Trends: Online Dating," http://cp.match .com/cppp/media/CMB_Study.pdf (accessed August 5, 2010).
3. Jim Liebelt, "Online Predators: Separating Fact and Fiction." Crosswalk.com, http://www.crosswalk.com/ parenting/11604906 (accessed August 5, 2010).

Chapter 5: Teaching the Purity Code

1. Jonathan Liew, "All Men Watch Porn, Scientists Find," Telegraph.co.uk, December 2, 2009, http://www.telegraph.co.uk/relationships/6709646/All-men-watch-porn-scientists-find.html (accessed August 5, 2010).

2. Rob Stein, "A Debunking on Teenagers and 'Technical Virginity,'" May 20, 2008, http://www.washingtonpost.com/wp-dyn/content/article/2008/05/19/AR2008051901219.html.

3. Michael D. Lemonick, "A Teen Twist on Sex," *Time*, September 19, 2005.

4. Jennifer Warner, "Exposure to Sexual Media Content May Prompt Teen Sex," FoxNews.com, April 3, 2005, http://www.foxnews.com/story/0,2933,190355,00.html (accessed August 5, 2010).

Chapter 6: Communication Is Key

1. Maya Angelou, *Singin' and Swingin' and Gettin' Merry Like Christmas* (New York: Random House, 2009), 41.

2. This prayer has been attributed to multiple authors, including Orin L. Crain and Wilferd A. Peterson.

3. Wayne Rice, *Cleared for Takeoff* (Nashville: Word, 2000), 139.

4. John Rosemond, *The Well-Behaved Child* (Nashville: Thomas Nelson, 2009), 25.

Chapter 7: The Spiritual Life of a Teenager

1. For a more thorough approach to the spiritual influences on teenagers, see the Search Institute study in Mark Holmen, *Building Faith at Home* (Ventura, CA: Regal Books, 2007), 26.

2. Christian Smith and Melinda Lundquist Denton, *Soul*

Searching: The Religious and Spiritual Lives of American Teenagers (New York: Oxford University Press, 2005), 56.

3. Wayne Rice, *Generation to Generation* (Cincinnati: Standard Publishing, 2010), 36.

4. Henri J. M. Nouwen, *Making All Things New* (New York: HarperCollins, 1981), 66.

5. You may want to check out my series of six *Family Time Faith Conversations* booklets that will be available in 2011. The titles include "A Strong Family," "Building Morals & Values," and "The Life of Jesus."

6. Christian Smith, "Theorizing Religious Effects Among American Adolescents," *Journal for the Scientific Study of Religion* 42:1 (2003) 17–30.

7. James W. Fowler, *Stages of Faith: The Psychology of Human Development* (New York: HarperCollins, 1981), 117–199.

Chapter 8: Dealing With a Troubled Teen

1. Ruth Bell Graham, *Collected Poems,* © 1998 The Ruth Graham Literary Trust. Used by permission. All rights reserved.

2. Many couples do have different parenting styles, and even more so in divorce situations, parents will have opposite philosophies. My suggestion is to do the best you can to form your parenting strategy, stick to it, and bring consistency whenever possible to the situation. Seek counsel when necessary.

3. Again, there are excellent resources out there to help you put a plan together and get on the same page. My book *Confident Parenting* helps parents put together a parenting philosophy that works and is scriptural; *Parenting Teens with Love and Logic* by Foster Cline and Jim Fay is an excellent resource for parenting philosophy and helping to follow a plan; and *The Well-Behaved Child* by John Rosemond provides

a solid philosophy of good parenting and training for your child to one day be a responsible adult.

4. For an example of a substance abuse questionnaire for parents, visit www.homeword.com.

Chapter 10: The Changing Culture

1. Tom McBride and Ron Nief, "The Mindset List," Beloit College, http://www.beloit.edu/mindset/ (accessed August 5, 2010).
2. Walt Mueller, "5 Truths About Pop Culture," The Center for Parent/Youth Understanding, https://www.cpyu.org/Page .aspx?id=77176 (accessed August 5, 2010).

Part Two: Common Problems and Solutions

1. Sean T. Carroll, et al., "Tattoos and Body-Piercings as Indicators of Adolescent Risk-Taking Behaviors," *Pediatrics* 109 (2002), 1021–1027.
2. Robin Kowalski, "You Wanna Take This Online?" *Time*, August 8, 2005.
3. Ibid.
4. Substance Abuse & Mental Health Services Administration, "Majority of America's 2 Million Adolescents Suffering from Depression Episodes Did Not Receive Treatment in the Past Year," news release, May 13, 2009, http://www.samhsa.gov/ newsroom/advisories/0905134443.aspx (accessed August 5, 2010).
5. American Academy of Child and Adolescent Psychiatry, "The Depressed Child," *Facts for Families* No. 4 (May 2008), http://www.aacap.org/galleries/FactsForFamilies/04_the _depressed_child.pdf (accessed August 5, 2010).
6. National Center on Addiction and Substance Abuse at Columbia University, "The Importance of Family Dinners V,"

press release, September 23, 2009, http://www.casacolumbia
.org/templates/PressReleases.aspx?articleid=567&zoneid=85
(accessed August 5, 2010).

7. S.A.F.E. (Self-Abuse Finally Ends) Alternatives is an excellent resource for self-injuring teens and their parents. For more information, visit their Web site at www.selfinjury.com.

8. Drexel University, "Teens Fueled by Caffeine Use Too Much Technology and Don't Get Enough Sleep Drexel Professor Finds," news release, July 20, 2009, http://drexel.edu/ news/headlines/teens-fueled-by-caffeine-use-too-much -technology-and-don't-get-enough-sleep-drexel-professor -finds.aspx (accessed August 5, 2010).

9. My mother used to quote an old Irish proverb: "A good laugh and a long sleep are the best cures in the doctor's book." Sounds like good advice for parents and their teens.

10. I deal with this issue in greater detail in my books *Teaching Your Children Healthy Sexuality* (for parents), *The Purity Code* (for ages 10 to 14), and *Accept Nothing Less* (for ages 14 and up).

11. John Rosemond, *Ending the Homework Hassle* (Kansas City, MO: Andrews and McMeel, 1990).

HOME HW WORD

WHERE PARENTS GET REAL ANSWERS

Get Equipped with HomeWord...

LISTEN
HomeWord Radio
programs reach over 800 communities nationwide with *HomeWord with Jim Burns* – a daily ½ hour interview feature, *HomeWord Snapshots* – a daily 1 minute family drama, and *HomeWord this Week* – a ½ hour weekend edition of the daily program, and our one-hour program.

CLICK
HomeWord.com
provides advice and resources to millions of visitors each year. A truly interactive website, HomeWord.com provides access to parent newsletter, Q&As, online broadcasts, tip sheets, our online store and more.

READ
HomeWord Resources
parent newsletters, equip families and Churches worldwide with practical Q&As, online broadcasts, tip sheets, our online store and more. Many of these resources are also packaged digitally to meet the needs of today's busy parents.

ATTEND
HomeWord Events
Understanding Your Teenager, Building Healthy Morals & Values, Generation 2 Generation and Refreshing Your Marriage are held in over 100 communities nationwide each year. HomeWord events educate and encourage parents while providing answers to life's most pressing parenting and family questions.

A Ministry with *Jim Burns*

In response to the overwhelming needs of parents and families, Jim Burns founded HomeWord in 1985. HomeWord, a Christian organization, equips and encourages parents, families, and churches worldwide.

Find Out More
Sign up for our FREE daily e-devotional and parent e-newsletter at HomeWord.com, or call 800.397.9725.

HomeWord.com

More From Jim Burns

Purity Is So Much More Than Abstinence—It's a Lifestyle.

Prepare Them for *Life*.

The PURE FOUNDATIONS resource line is a biblical, straightforward approach to help parents and youth leaders instill godly values about relationships, identity, sex, and sexuality in today's young people.

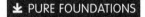

⬇ PURE FOUNDATIONS

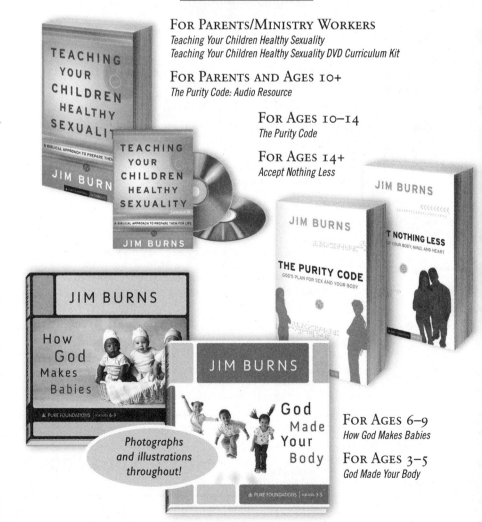

FOR PARENTS/MINISTRY WORKERS
Teaching Your Children Healthy Sexuality
Teaching Your Children Healthy Sexuality DVD Curriculum Kit

FOR PARENTS AND AGES 10+
The Purity Code: Audio Resource

FOR AGES 10–14
The Purity Code

FOR AGES 14+
Accept Nothing Less

FOR AGES 6–9
How God Makes Babies

FOR AGES 3–5
God Made Your Body

Photographs and illustrations throughout!